# Traditional Dyeing

# Traditional Dyeing

by
Lynn Huggins-Cooper

PEN & SWORD HISTORY

AN IMPRINT OF PEN & SWORD BOOKS LTD.
YORKSHIRE - PHILADELPHIA

First published in Great Britain in 2022 by
Pen & Sword History
An imprint of
Pen & Sword Books Ltd
Yorkshire – Philadelphia

ISBN 978 1 52672 456 4

Typeset in Ehrhardt 12/17 by
SJmagic DESIGN SERVICES, India.
Printed and bound in the UK by CPI Group (UK) Ltd, Croydon, CR0 4YY.

Pen & Sword Books Limited incorporates the imprints of Atlas, Archaeology,
Aviation, Discovery, Family History, Fiction, History, Maritime, Military,
Military Classics, Politics, Select, Transport, True Crime, Air World,
Frontline Publishing, Leo Cooper, Remember When, Seaforth Publishing,
The Praetorian Press, Wharncliffe Local History, Wharncliffe Transport,
Wharncliffe True Crime and White Owl.

For a complete list of Pen & Sword titles please contact

PEN & SWORD BOOKS LIMITED
47 Church Street, Barnsley, South Yorkshire, S70 2AS, England
E-mail: enquiries@pen-and-sword.co.uk
Website: www.pen-and-sword.co.uk

Or
PEN AND SWORD BOOKS
1950 Lawrence Rd, Havertown, PA 19083, USA
E-mail: Uspen-and-sword@casematepublishers.com
Website: www.penandswordbooks.com

# Contents

# Introduction to Heritage Crafts

Heritage crafts are a part of what makes us who we are; part of the glue that has held families and communities together for centuries. That jumper your nanna knitted – a heritage craft. The willow basket made by your auntie – a heritage craft. Grandpa's hand-turned pipe – again, a heritage craft. These traditional crafts have been carried out for centuries, often handed down through families with a child learning the craft at a parent's knee. Heritage crafts are those traditional crafts that are a part of the customs and cultural heritage of the areas where they begin. A heritage craft is:

> a practice which employs manual dexterity and skill and an understanding of traditional materials, design and techniques, and which has been practised for two or more successive generations.

Radcliffe Red List of Endangered Crafts Report, Heritage Crafts Association 2017.

Heritage crafts are in trouble. The Heritage Crafts Association commissioned research into endangered crafts, supported by The Radcliffe Trust (http://theradcliffetrust.org/). The results make sobering reading. Greta Bertram, Secretary of the Heritage Crafts Association who led the research said:

> The Radcliffe Red List of Endangered Crafts is the first research of its kind in the UK. We're all familiar with the idea

of a red list of endangered species, but this is the first time the methodology has been applied to our intangible craft heritage. While some crafts are indeed thriving, the research has shown that all crafts, and not just those identified as critically endangered, face a wide range of challenges to their long-term survival. When any craft is down to the last few makers it has to be considered at risk as an unpredicted twist of fate can come at any time.

Some of the heritage crafts identified in the report are teetering on the brink of disaster, and could be lost during this generation. One hundred and sixty-nine crafts were surveyed, and were allocated a status of currently viable, endangered, critically endangered or extinct. The survey team spoke to craft organisations and craftspeople, heritage professionals and funding bodies, as well as members of the public.

Four crafts surveyed were seen as already extinct, having been lost in the last ten years: riddle and sieve making; cricket ball making; gold beating; and lacrosse stick making. In 2019, mould and deckle making was added to the list.

Ian Keys, Chair of the Heritage Crafts Association, said

We would like to see the Government recognise the importance of traditional craft skills as part of our cultural heritage, and take action to ensure they are passed on to the next generation. Craft skills today are in the same position that historic buildings were a hundred years ago – but we now recognise the importance of old buildings as part of our heritage, and it's time for us to join the rest of the world and recognise that these living cultural traditions are just as important and need safeguarding too.

An alarming thirty-seven more crafts (as at 2021) are seen by the report as critically endangered, and at serious risk. There are few artisans practising the crafts – sometimes there are just one or two businesses operating – and there are few or no trainees learning the craft anew as apprentices. So why do we find ourselves in this situation? At a time when a huge variety of crafts are enjoyed as a hobby is booming, and craft fairs pop up in every community centre, village hall and historic estate, it seems odd that traditional crafts are dying out. So why is there a problem?

The study found that for some of the endangered crafts, there was an ageing workforce with nobody young training, waiting in the wings to take over. For others, there were found to be few training courses, even if there were potential trainees. For some traditional crafters, the problem was found to be a variety of economic factors. Cheap competing crafts from overseas have flooded the market, and there is often an unwillingness on the part of the public to pay a fair price for items handmade in Britain, despite the craftsmanship involved and the high quality of products. Of course, most traditional craftspeople are running microbusinesses, and it is increasingly difficult to run a small business in Britain with an increase in paperwork, red tape, rules and regulations. Add to the quantity of bureaucratic tasks and marketing necessary for self-employment and that leaves scant time for honing and practising an artisanal craft.

Three crafts that are part of the leather-making and tanning industry have been identified as critically endangered: tanning with oak bark; parchment and vellum making; and collar making, for heavy horses and harness driving. 'Critical' status means, according to the study, that there is a shrinking number of craftspeople carrying out the craft, and that there are limited training opportunities for those wanting to enter the craft. It means that entering the craft has limited financial viability. Today, for example, oak bark tanning by hand on an industrial scale is only carried out by one producer in Britain: J. & F.J. Baker & Co. Ltd in Devon.

Despite producing finer, stronger leather than chemical production, such as chrome tanning, this mode of production is expensive due to the time taken and is only used for high-end products. Rightly so; the process of tanning is a slow, meditative process. The bark itself is dried for two to three years before being crushed for use, and the entire process of oak bark tanning may take up to fourteen months.

The future of heritage crafts is threatened in Great Britain. Action needs to be taken now to reverse the trend and ensure that these heritage cultural traditions are not lost forever. So far, we are failing. Great Britain is one of only 22 countries out of 194 to not have ratified the 2003 UNESCO Convention on the Safeguarding of Intangible Cultural Heritage. This convention focuses on the non-physical aspects of heritage such as traditional festivals, oral traditions, performing arts and the knowledge and skills to produce traditional crafts. If governmental action is not taken soon, many heritage crafts will be consigned to history.

You can help by supporting heritage craftworkers with your wallet, and by attending demonstrations and events. You can also join the Heritage Crafts Association, even if you are not a heritage crafter yourself, to support the funding and research of heritage craft practices. At the time of writing in 2021, it is £20 for an individual to join. http://heritagecrafts.org.uk/get-involved/

*Chapter 1*

# Introduction to Traditional Dyeing

P eople have always loved colour. It's one of the greatest pleasures in life – we marvel at the watercolour wash of a dawn sky or the vibrant shades of sunset as it fades to twilight; we love the glittering azure or the stormy grey of the sea and the tones both vivid and muted of our landscapes. Then the colours of the flora and fauna of our beautiful world – the russet of squirrel and deer – and autumn leaves; the yellows from buttery flowers to acidic coloured fruits; the wash of a scarlet poppy field in full bloom and the deep plum of – well, ripe plums! Shades of green can range from the near fluorescent acid of newly unfurled leaves, to the deep pine green of the forest. Colour is everywhere!

It is no wonder that humans from the earliest times have used colour to brighten themselves and their surroundings. The earliest cave paintings used ochres from the earth to make art, for example. For as long as there has been cloth to make clothes and furnishings, people have been dyeing them. At first, people used natural dyes, experimenting with berries, earth colours, plant materials, tree bark and more. Some of these colours started bright, but quickly faded as the dyes were *fugitive* and did not stain the cloth permanently. As people settled and turned from hunter gathering to farming, dye plants were grown and used domestically for a long time. Over time, experimentation added mordant to fix the dyes and make them permanent. Eventually as commerce began to grow, so did the dye trade. Merchants imported exotic dyes from overseas, and the dye trade became a lucrative business.

Dyes have been made down the centuries from everything from beetles, such as cochineal and kermes, to plant roots such as madder, to leaves such as woad, and flowers such as marigolds. Reading old recipes can put one in mind of sorcery and spells, and witches' brews – and it makes for fascinating yet informative reading.

Dyes have made fortunes; the wealth they created have strengthened and enriched crowns and empires. Dyes have been responsible for slavery and terrible health risks and effects, and a great deal of environmental damage in more recent times, from the Victorian era onwards.

Dyes and their invention have driven the development of whole industries, and have even been responsible for amazing scientific discoveries and health care opportunities, such as disinfectants. The chemical industry that grew up from the use of coal tar in the Victorian era engendered change at a societal level, bringing bright colours within the reach of the poorer classes in society, and creating access to cheaper, mass produced and dyed cloth under the factory system, largely destroying cottage industries overnight. These chemical dyes also damaged the watercourses and created pollution and caused terrible sickness and untold deaths. Commercial dyes are still generally chemically based today – and whilst dreadful stories come to light on a far too regular basis about poor and dangerous working conditions for dye and textile production workers in developing countries, the industry as a whole is safe and well regulated.

However, despite the decimation of the natural dyes industry as it was superseded by cheap chemical dyes and industrialisation, the knowledge gathered by the natural dyers down the centuries was not lost. Today, modern 'cottage industries' are the leaders in innovative use of dye plants and other materials to create gloriously dyed fibre and fabric, and I had the privilege of interviewing modern day artisans for this book. Eco dyeing, solar dyeing and more can be discovered in their testimonies to their wonderful work. Artisans around the world are planting and harvesting dye gardens, processing great vats of fermenting indigo, and using plant materials to create beautiful fibre, yarn and fabric.

Natural dyeing is rather more complex than the beautiful but rather misleading posts of bright berries and flowers on social media would have you believe, however seductive are their sumptuous botanical photographs saturated with colour. Modern artisans using natural dyes (such as some of the amazing textile artists interviewed for this book) use two types of natural dyes. Firstly, there are the additive dyes such as madder that use a fixative or mordant to allow the dye to bond with fibres. Mordants can be weak organic acids such as tannic acid and acetic acid. They can also be metal salts such as alum, ferrous sulphate and copper sulphate. The textiles are soaked and simmered in mordant solution (known as pre-mordanting) before the dyes are applied. In other techniques, mordant is added to the dyebath or a mordant is applied to the textile after dyeing to change the colour result. These types of dyes have been used for more than 2,000 years.

Substantive dyes such as cochineal from beetles, safflower and black walnut on the other hand are able to bond with fibre without the use of a mordant – or they may in fact contain tannin which acts as a natural fixative or mordant.

Some natural dyes are what are known as *polychromic* which means they have the almost magical property of yielding different colours with different mordants. Cochineal and madder are in the polychromic category of dyes.

Natural dyeing is growing again in popularity and even in commercial settings. This is as a response to modern ecological concerns about 'stepping lightly on the earth' and producing vibrant colours without sacrificing the environment. Natural dyes are renewable and their development as a growing industry can offer a contribution to the rural economy and regeneration and diversification. Although modern synthetic dyes are available in a fantastic range of colours, and in strong shades, modern applications of traditional natural dyes can produce results with excellent colour fastness, depth of shades and a real sense of achievement for the artisans developing these amazing products.

This book is a mere whistle-stop tour of dyes in different periods of history and hopefully the reader will discover some interesting gems and ideas along the way. As well as a historical tour through colours for textiles, there are fascinating windows, generously given, by top-class artisans working in the field today. Using many historical methods, they have adapted and experimented to make these methods their own. These pioneers bring with them the techniques, methods and well-researched ideas from the past and bring them up to date with stunning, deliciously coloured results as you will see from photographs of their work included here.

I have also included, for the *dye curious*, some activities to dip your toes as it were into these colourful and often fragrant (or pungent!) waters. You can, by spending just a few pounds, try eco dyeing with plant treasures gathered on walks around your home, or even from your garden. It truly feels like alchemy when you take plant leaves, flowers and fronds, and wrap them in mordanted fabric before steaming them in your kitchen. The excitement of snipping the strings and unwinding your fabric to reveal the glorious prints hidden inside is a unique thrill – and highly addictive. Eco dyeing is a contemplative and exciting experience and connects you to the place where you collect the plant materials. As such, you can make meaningful art with a sense of place or even time – what an amazing way to make a memento of a wedding, special birthday or more. Eco-dyed fabric can be used for scarves and other items of clothing, but also to bind or cover journals or photograph albums – magical.

I have also added information on starting your own small-scale dyer's garden, and added details of places to buy seed and dye plants. Even a small bed of dye plants in a border will give you plenty of exciting materials such as coreopsis, weld, woad or madder to play with. Have a go and see what amazing colours you can achieve with plants you have raised yourself from seed; a truly satisfying artistic experience.

You can follow the progress of my own dye garden on my fibre and felting page on Facebook at www.facebook.com/EntertheWildwoods and on my website at EntertheWildwoods.co.uk. So – come with me and explore the colourful, magical world of dyeing!

*Chapter 2*

# Ancient Dyeing

From the most ancient of times, people have used the colour of dyes to adorn themselves and their surroundings. From clothes, to furnishings and even hair, we have always loved decorating our lives, peacock-like, with flashes of colour.

Pompeii, the city paradoxically destroyed *and* preserved by the eruption of Mount Vesuvius, gives us a fascinating insight into the range of colours and their applications that were available to the people who lived there, so many centuries ago. The volcanic eruption that tragically stilled so many people as they went about their everyday lives, has given us a unique snapshot of life in ancient times. Frescos uncovered in excavations at Pompeii show us that far from the popular portrayal of classical white robes, colour was a valued part of everyday dress in this sophisticated ancient centre of trade. Portrayals of women wearing differing shades of blues and greens show that although easily available materials such as lichen may have been used, it is more likely that vivid imported dyes such as indigo for example were employed to cater for the need for more reliable colours for the latest fashions.

The palette of colours available from plant based dyes was largely similar to those found in remains from many other countries at the time. Dyers in Pompeii used the usual madder for reds, woad for blue shades and a variety of berries, petals and tree barks were also used.

They were, however a busy centre for trade, and this meant they were exposed to rarer more exotic imported colours. Trade routes between the Roman Empire and India probably helped to introduce dyes such as indigo to the dye vats of Pompeii. Trade between the Empire and India can be evidenced in the excavations of the area which revealed an amazing carved idol of Lakshmi, the Hindu goddess of wealth and purity. This was found in a shrine in one of the houses in Pompeii. Archaeologists have also found evidence of a great deal of fine textile production in the preserved way of life in the shadow of Vesuvius – so it would have been surprising if fine dyes as well as luxurious fibres had not been in evidence in the rich way of life uncovered in Pompeii.

It is interesting for students of dyeing textiles to note that in Pompeii it seems from the evidence that it was unlikely that dyers would wait for a garment to be finished in the maker's chosen material, and then apply a dye to it. It is thought that it was far more commonplace for the dye to be applied to the material itself while in a raw state. For example wool would be dyed as a fleece before it was spun in a similar manner that the wools used in felting or coloured yarn are dyed before being used today.

References to the vivid variety of colours available in the ancient world can be found in accounts recorded by poets and philosophers of the time. We can, from their writings, find a window into a nuanced and meaning-filled world of colour. The record shows that colours were both valued and valuable at this time; that they held meaning and that thought and scholarship was devoted to these ideas.

The extraordinary lengths taken to produce certain colours are astonishing to modern eyes (and perhaps a somewhat dubious testimony to the use of slave labour and meagre wages in the ancient world!). Some dyes took far more effort to obtain than others. Purple, ever a royal colour, was produced from a rather unlikely source. Gorgeous purple dye required a slimy defensive chemical secreted by certain sea snails. To produce even a small amount of the dye would require thousands of these snails to be collected, and crushed in order to collect enough of the material. Vastly resource and labour intensive, it is little wonder then that this colour was expensive. Purple fabric would have been seen draped across the richest and most powerful citizens of ancient Rome, for example, such as the Emperor. As with all natural dyes, it is important to note that the colours produced by this process would vary in the production process. Indeed, different shades obtained over time from these snails in the ancient world have been known as *Tyrian Purple*, *Phoenician Purple* and *Imperial Purple*.

Tyrian Purple was thus called because of its origins in Tyre, a sophisticated Phoenician city in the Bronze Age. With hues that ranged from red to purple, Tyrian Purple resisted fading, and, it is said, became even more intense as a colour with wear - but was complex and costly to manufacture. This kept its price high – and made it an attractive status symbol. Only the very wealthy could afford clothes created with this exquisite dyestuff. Shades produced varied from a rich crimson to a purple so deep it was almost black. Tyrian Purple was a truly premium dye product, and the Phoenicians were experts in blending the secretions of the few different types of shellfish used to create the dye, using closely guarded trade secrets and processes, and adding secret ingredients. Arguably the most prized purple in the ancient world, Tyrian Purple was a deep, rich shade that was flooded with a crimson glow when it was held up to the sunlight.

A lovely story recorded in Phoenician mythology is that the idea for the process for extracting the vivid purple dye from molluscs came from a simple dog walk. Tyre's patron god *Melqart* was said to have had a mistress called *Tyros*. She had a pet dog (we are not told *his* name), and was walking with him along the shore when the playful dog came upon a Murex, picking it up and carrying it for a time along the beach in his mouth, staining its muzzle purple in the process. Tyros loved the colour (no doubt looking rather rakish on her pup) and asked her lover for a gorgeous garment to be made using the glorious, rich purple dye – and thus, the story goes, an entire lucrative industry was born.

Interestingly, a similar tale is told in the myths of the Ancient Greeks – perhaps as a result of trade between the civilisations sharing stories as well as goods. According to Julius Pollux writing in the second century, purple was stumbled upon by a dog, as in the Phoenician myth. However, this time the dog belonged to Heracles the demigod and son of Zeus. In this tale, Heracles was travelling to meet with a beloved nymph, when his pup chewed on a snail along the shore. Again, when the lovely lady saw the colour on the dog's fur, she desired it for herself – perhaps even overshadowing her desire for her beau. She asked for a robe to be made for her of the same colour. The scene is immortalised in the seventeenth-century painting *Hercules' Dog Discovers Purple Dye* by the Flemish master Peter Paul Rubens. The oil painting shows the wrong sort of shellfish – it is not the spiky Murex that produced Tyrian Purple; instead a whimsical coiled shell – but it is interesting to see all the same.

A charming tale – but we have documented proof that shows us that there is a record of the dye dating back to at least the fourteenth century BCE. Ugarit and Hittite sources describe the production of the famous dye, and detail the success of the export and the wealth it created. Some historians have even claimed that the very name *Phoenicia* may have been derived from the Greek word *phoinos*, which means dark red – and that this in turn may be derived from the Akkadian word for red, *kinahhu*.

As new discoveries are made, we can often find that certain dyes, and even the means for producing them may have existed a long time before we initially suspected. Phoenician Purple may well be among them. An investigation into the suspected site of a Minoan dye works showed evidence of crushed Murex shells being present. The site in question was thought to date around 1,700 years before the Common Era, suggesting that the colour may have existed around 130 years before its Phoenician fame, and there is some record of Minoan production on a small scale at least on tablets from Knossos. Indeed, given the coastal nature and aptitude for seafaring of both civilisations, it is entirely possible that the Phoenicians of Tyre procured their ability to create the sought-after purple dye from the Minoans themselves on one of their voyages to trade – or perhaps a Minoan shipmaster passed on the knowledge when in a Phoenician port. Maybe they developed their processes independently. Whatever the truth of the initial development of the dye, the Phoenicians became famed as the manufacturers and traders of the source of this glorious colour, and they exported it to many areas including Carthage, where it may have first been seen by the acquisitive eyes of Roman society. In the Roman Empire, *Tyrian* (later known as *Imperial*) *Purple* would become a symbol of the authority and status of the Emperor.

Tyrian Purple was extracted from several shellfish. Apart from the main source, *Murex brandaris*, the purple fluid could also be extracted from *Murex trunculus*, *Helix ianthina* and *Purpura lapillus*. Fishermen would sail out into deep waters and lay baited traps for the shellfish which they suspended by floats to make them easy to find and haul the valuable shells back to shore. The shells of the unfortunate creatures were crushed and laid out in the sun to bake and dry. The smell of the putrefying shellfish must have been powerful, and a far cry from the expensive and desirable cloth it would dye. The liquid produced would be used to produce dyes that varied from deep violet to blush pink. The purple comes from the shellfish's defence response and interestingly is colourless when fresh, but darkens as it dries and is exposed to air.

Some 10,000 shellfish were needed to produce 1g of dye – a stunning fact borne out by the huge quantities of shells found in massive heaps at a site in Sidon, which created a mountain an astonishing 40 metres high! So many shellfish were gathered that the species used were nearly driven to extinction in the ancient world – a sobering early example of greed leading to the impoverishing of the natural environment.

Pliny the Elder, in his opus *Natural History*, wrote about the dye extraction process used to create Tyrian Purple. He wrote about the mashed shellfish glands being salted and boiled in tins to produce dye liquor. Fleeces were then immersed in the liquid to absorb the colour. The dyed fibres were combed and spun, and woven into cloth. Clothes were then made. It was rare, according to Pliny, for finished items of clothing to be dyed, although some very precious and costly pieces may have been redyed for a deeper shade once they were complete.

Tyrian Purple was also produced in Lesbos, Rhodes, Kerkouane in Northern Africa and Motya in Sicily. It was used primarily to dye a high-quality fine fabric known as *Dibapha* meaning twice dipped. It produced a rich and deep shaded and luxurious cloth which naturally became a status symbol which carried great prestige. The high value of the cloth is displayed by the records that remain, showing that it was an important part of tribute lists (along with precious metals such as gold and silver) paid by Tyre to the Assyrian kings in the ninth and eighth centuries BCE. Whilst purple could be produced from lichens, or by overdyeing madder cloth (a shade of red) with woad dye (a shade of blue), or by berries (for example, the whortleberries used by Gaulish dyers) – Tyrian Purple was the most desirable.

In Roman society, Imperial Purple was the property of the elite – the highest echelons of society. In ancient Rome, only magistrates and the Imperial family were permitted to wear the *toga praetexta*, which had a purple border. Feted generals celebrating a Triumph were permitted the honour of the *toga picta*, which was a sumptuous purple toga bordered with gold – truly magnificent! Over time, purple came to be associated with the Emperor alone. Julius Caesar wore the *toga purpurea*, an all-purple garment of great status. A price edict dating from the time of the Emperor Diocletian in 301 CE tells us that a pound of purple dye fetched a price of 150, 000 denarii – the equivalent of 3 pounds of gold. A costly dye indeed!

In Ancient Greece, the right to wear purple was enshrined in law. Only citizens of the highest rank were permitted to wear purple. According to the Roman historian Suetonius, it was the wearing of purple on a visit to the mad and cruel Roman Emperor Caligula that cost king Ptolemy of Mauretania his life. Caligula saw the wearing of purple as an affront to his own position of power and status, and an act of aggression – and had poor unfortunate Ptolemy killed.

Tyrian Purple was used in other ways than textiles; it was occasionally used to dye important parchment. From Late antiquity, the Codex Rossano survives into the modern day.

It is interesting to note additionally that relatively recently, a new perspective on colours used in sculpture has emerged. In the same way as with clothing, the commonly accepted idea of all Roman and Greek sculpture being of pure white marble was most likely incorrect. By examining tool marks made on classical sculptures, archaeologists have been able to determine that there were layers of rich colours applied to statues in order to give them a true to life appearance. Over time through natural wear and in the case of those items kept outside, the elements, have worn down the colour, exposing the white marble beneath which led to the widely accepted view that pure white marble was the standard. As more research has been conducted to confirm this, there have been many documents uncovered discussing the difficulty that Roman artisans had in protecting the colour on statues and sculpture and there have even been pieces found that depict artists colouring their works.

Within certain cultures, as we have seen in Ancient Rome, Ancient Greece and Phoenicia, some colours can take on a more significant meaning than purely their aesthetic quality. As previously discussed Phoenician Purple indicated wealth and therefore high status due to its costly production methods. In some societies, however, colours convey meaning that is not necessarily related to its associated cost.

The ancient Egyptians believed that colour conveyed meaning so much so that the translation of the word for colour – *Iwn* – can also be translated to mean *nature* or *disposition*. Yellow and gold were thought to represent things that would last forever and had connections to the sun god *Ra*. This may partly be due to the fact that gold was thought to be the skin of the gods themselves. This idea, as well as its incipient value, is part of the reason that the coffins of pharaohs were so heavily decorated with gold, as well as funereal masks: death for a pharaoh meant ascension to godhood.

White was often associated with religious ceremony and the priesthood and because of its representation of purity and was often considered the counter colour to red which represented anger and violence. The colours created to be used in paints and dyes by the Egyptians were often derived from iron oxides and other mineral compounds, as well as ochres. Some arsenic was used for creation of yellows and greens in slightly later eras. However, the usual natural colour sources of madder and indigo have also been found to have been in use through archaeological digs. In Ancient Egypt, only one boat had an indigo-purple sail, and that belonged to Pharoah. It was a sign for other sailors on the River Nile to move aside as their great ruler was among them.

A particularly interesting find when it comes to dyeing in ancient Egypt was discovered in Antinooupolis in around 1913 by an English archaeologist working on behalf of the Egypt Exploration Fund. Despite the common image of ancient Egyptians barefoot or in sandals, while excavating the city, an example of a coloured striped sock was found. Through modern digital analysis, scientists have come to understand that the yarn in a striped sock had been exposed to multiple dye baths in order to produce the different coloured stripes. As well as this, some fibres had been spun together in order to blend them. Sampling of the sock showed the use of madder, weld and woad to achieve the red, yellow and blue respectively within the sock and dating has shown the sock to have been produced around 300 CE. The advanced knitting techniques used to create this particular example of a sock makes it stand out, and it is a fascinating piece. The sock was given to the British Museum in 1914 and remains part of their collection today.

The rich blue of indigo dye was known across the ancient world, and is one of the oldest dyes known and recorded for use in the dyeing and printing of textiles. The oldest known example of indigo dye being used to colour fabric was discovered by archaeologists in Peru. A dig excavating the temple at Huaca Prieta, near Trujillo in Peru discovered pieces of fabric dyed with indigo, as well as ochre. These pieces of fabric are thought to be between 4,000 and 6,200 years old, which identifies them as the oldest known surviving example of indigo being used to dye fabric.

Indigo has a rich history as a dyestuff, and examples have been found in digs of Mesopotamian sites. A neo–Babylonian tablet from the seventh century BCE offers a recipe and process for the dyeing of wool with indigo. It describes a deep lapis lazuli shade of blue, which was produced by the repeated immersion of wool in the dye bath. Indigo was also found in investigations of the archaeological sites of the Ancient Britons. Mesoamerican digs and African sites show that indigo was found across the globe in the ancient world. The Ancient Greeks and Romans also used indigo as a luxury dye, and Romans used indigo as a colour in paintings and murals, and for dazzling cosmetics and even for medicinal purposes. It was brought to the Mediterranean by Arab merchants.

In India, Japan and across South East Asia, indigo has been used as a silk dye for hundreds of years. *Indigofera Tinctoria* was domesticated and farmed in India from early times. In fact, the antiquity of indigo as a product of India is perhaps best shown by the association between the Greek word for the dye *indikon*, and the Latinized word used by the Romans, *indicum*. This became *indigo*.

The lovely red dye produced from madder root (*Rubia Tinctorum*) also has its origins in the ancient world. The ancient Egyptians, Greeks and Romans used it to dye textiles. Madder has been grown and farmed in central Asia from as early as 1,500 BCE. Cloth dyed with madder was found in the ruined remains of Pompeii, in ancient Corinth and even in the tomb of the pharaoh Tutankhamun in Egypt.

So, in the ancient world colour was valued; dyeing was a valued skill and the colours worn by different strata of society displayed their wealth and status (or lack of it). Colour had meaning and some dyes were costly and valuable – and labour-intensive to produce. There has been a resurgence of interest in ancient dyes amongst modern artisans, and it will be interesting to see where this leads us in terms of natural colour production. Exciting times!

*Chapter 3*

# Medieval Traditional Dyeing

In the medieval era, much of the knowledge gained in ancient times continued to be used, and in some places, developed further. Many people produced their own limited palette of dyes at home. To an extent, colours worn were still seen as denoting status and class. Bright, expensive colours were not seen as suitable for the lower peasant class by societal rules. Bright colours were seen as lacking somehow in the humility expected of peasants. Peasants inhabited a lowly space and were expected to recognise that and stay firmly where society put them. If God created them as peasants, any attempt to change their position (including, fascinatingly to modern sensibilities, wearing bright colours) was seen as flying in the face of the natural order and going against God's will. Isn't it amazing that God's will aligned with the needs and wants of the rich? Bright colours were seen as engendering pride; a mortal sin. Interestingly this did not apply to the higher classes in society.

The colour and brightness of dye helped to determine its value. The production of dyes was complex and the processes involved were often unpleasant and smelly (as some natural dye processes are even today!). The demand for dyes increased year upon year and in 1472, Edward IV incorporated the Dyers' Company of London – so we see the growth of the industry and its importance at this time.

The lower classes were expected to wear drab, dull colours, no doubt to ensure they remained in the background, ready to do the bidding of their 'betters'. Muted greys, browns and blues were often worn by the lower classes. Luckily, these colours were easily available and could be produced from local plant materials.

Medieval rural housewives dyed the material they spun and wove. In the towns, fabrics could often be bought ready woven and dyed, and travelling merchants took fabrics around the country in packs to sell. Housewives planted dye plants in their gardens in order to carry out these domestic duties, and richer households purchased expensive, strong and bright dye from exotic international supplies.

Madder root (*Rubia Tinctorum*) made red; this root was harvested once a year so even though it was a domestically available dye it was still fairly expensive to produce. More expensive, deeper reds were created from kermes or grana, which were imported insect based dyes.

To make blue dye, woad was extracted from the leaves of *Isatis Tinctoria*, and the leaves could be harvested several times each year, making it somewhat cheaper to produce than madder with its once yearly harvest.

Brown was produced from walnut bark and shells; green from weld and turmeric and violet, called *orchil*, from lichen. Yellow was derived from Dyer's Rocket, turmeric, saffron, marigold, chamomile, and onion skin. Purple dye came from brasilwood, from the East India Tree.

Flanders was in medieval times a hub for the production of fabric production and the dyeing of cloth (and the supply of dyestuff). Their soil was rich and deep, and ideal for growing the often large herbaceous plants that yielded dyes. Of course, it also had an abundant supply of the fine clay Fuller's earth, used extensively at the time in the cleansing and preparation of wool fleeces ready for spinning and weaving.

An amazing text dating from Germany in 1330, the *Innsbruck Manuscript* contained a wide variety of instructions for medieval dyers. Some of the recipes sound archaic and sometimes bizarre in terms of ingredients, but their tenets still hold up well today. The following extracts give some fascinating examples.

<u>To make yellow</u>, readers were told:

> Whosoever wishes to make yellow dye, takes orpiment and mixes it with alum, cooked in lime water, and dyes therewith.
>
> One should take barberries and peel the outer rind off; then one should peel off the green and boil it with alumwater and add brasilwood thereto and orpiment and dye therewith.

<u>For red</u>:

> Take chalk in a pot and pour water thereon and mix it well together and let it sink to the bottom of the pot so that the water becomes clear and take that same water and boil the brasilwood well therein, until it is cooked and then mix in alum and with it dye red zendel (a thin silken material).
>
> Whoever wants to dye whatsoever he wills red, takes cinnabar and rubs it well on a hard stone with alum-water and uses that to dye with. If he wants to make a red colour darker, he mixes it with black dye or with verdigris and adds alum thereto; then he cooks everything in lime water and takes brasilwood and boils everything in human urine.
>
> Also, brasilwood mixed with alum, mixed with lime water or with urine.
>
> One should take lead oxide and should boil it with lime water/vinegar, upon which the colour becomes the colour of tiles, and should mix it with alum, and a flower in the field named zindlot should also be boiled in alum-water and strain it through a cloth, and dye therewith.
>
> One should take crabs and boil them well in water and throw out of the pot everything within the shells and boil the rest.

Grind well in a mortar, and strain through a cloth and mix it well with alum, upon which the colour becomes reddish; or if one wishes to make the colour darker, add verdigris thereto.

Take brasilwood and maple as much as you wish and boil it well in lime water and take then alum and gum arabic thereto, so the brasilwood and the maple are well cooked, then let the alum and gum arabic seeth together, and therewith colour red upon white.

### For blue:

Whoever wishes to make a fast blue, take ground lapis lazuli colour in lime water and boil it with gum arabic and with alum and dye therewith. If he wishes to make it dark, add black dye thereto and blue flowers which stand in the field, and mash it well and boil it in urine and mix it with alum and dye therewith.

Take the leaves of a dwarf elder and mash them and take indigo and add thereto and grind it together and let them dry together for a long time and take lime water and let it seethe together and then take alum and grind it thereto while it's all hot. Paint it on white fabric, and it will become a good blue.

### For brown:

Take filings and rusty iron and soft pitch, and let it boil long together; that makes a good brown on a red fabric.

### For green:

To make a green dye, take verdigris and boil it in urine and mix alum thereto and a portion of gum arabic, and dye therewith;

to make the colour lighter, take this same colour and add orpiment and mix it with alum, cooked in lime water and dye therewith.

One should take elder and boil it in alumwater, that makes a green colour and also a black, if one mixes it with a bit of black colour.

For black:

Take green nutshells and grind them together and let them rot seven days in a pot, and therewith make a black dye.

Whoever wants to make black dye, he takes oak galls and pulverizes them and adds alum thereto and boils it in a skilful way with alum and in urine and dyes therewith; if he wants to make it darker, add black dye thereto.

As can be seen from the preparations described in the manuscript, medieval dyers were aware of the need for mordant and fixatives to improve colour permanence and ensure that dyed fabric stayed colourfast and lightfast, using *alumwater* extensively. This alum was imported by the year 1200 from North Africa, and Sicily. Alum was used both in dye baths and as a pre-mordant. It brightened colours, but using too much could make wool fibres 'sticky' – so these clever medieval dyers found a solution. They used tartaric acid to counteract the effect. Archaeological finds from Coppergate in York have taught us that *club moss* was used as an alternative to mined alum as a mordant in dyeing. One has to wonder at the brilliance that led to the discovery of the usefulness of this humble plant which we, in the modern day, can tell is high in naturally occurring alum. This was incredibly useful when mined alum was expensive and could be hard to obtain due to its imported nature.

Medieval dyers also used iron, often in the form of a post-dye bath, to tone and darken down colours – much like a modern day artisan would use the technique today. Another commonly used metal based mordant was copper, which often added a lovely blue/green cast to colours, and this was often facilitated by dyeing in a copper pot – ingenious!

Ammonia – readily found in urine, often collected for the purpose – was used to tinker with dye acidity levels, and alter shades and colours produced from plant materials such as woad and madder. Medieval dyers were inventive and took the craft almost to the level of alchemy, with their experimental pots and potions. Many dyes at this time were still costly to produce, and the processes labour (and resource) intensive. Precious dyes were carried across the world by traders, and not just via caravans on the ancient Silk Roads. Maritime technological advances such as the development of the science of navigation, and the improvement of shipbuilding techniques facilitated long distance sea travel. Coastal cities grew up around ports in places such as Zanzibar, Goa, Alexandria and these lively places were teeming with merchants bringing 'exotic' goods, including dyestuff, from the Far East. Thus, dyes and new techniques for dyeing – because ideas, languages and beliefs travelled along these routes as well as material goods – spread around the world and eventually into Europe. These would be added over time to the wealth of knowledge about dyeing already held in great houses, monasteries and humble homes.

*Chapter 4*

# Tudor and Stuart Traditional Dyeing

I n the Tudor and Elizabethan era, dyes were created from natural sources such as plants. The colours worn still denoted status and wealth; the darker and brighter colours were the province of the wealthy. Cheaper dyes were made from lichen (green shades), madder (red and pink shades), woad (blue shades) and weld (yellow shades). Lichen was gathered from trees and rocks.

In England, woad (*Isatis Tinctoria*), madder (*Rubia Tinctorum*) and weld (*Reseda Luteola*) were widely cultivated for dye production. Other materials such as lichen were foraged. The wealthy could of course buy imported dyes and dyed cloth.

## Natural materials used for dyeing
### Orchils (Lichen)
These tufted growths found on the bark of trees, rocks and rough ground were used to make shades of green (and sometimes purple) dye. They could be easily gathered for processing and were widely available.

This process describing how to produce purple dye from lichen is from 1540, from the Venetian Giovanni Ventura Rosetti, and was detailed in his work *Plichto dell'arte de Tintori*:

> Take one pound of Orselle of the Levant, very clean; moisten it with a little urine; add to this sal-ammoniac, sal-gemmae, and saltpetre, of each two ounces; pound them well, mix them together, and let them remain so during twelve days, stirring

them twice a day; and then to keep the herb constantly moist, add a little urine, and in this situation let it remain eight days longer, continuing to stir it; you afterwards add a pound and a half of pot-ash well pounded, and a pint and a half of stale urine. Let it remain still eight days longer, stirring it as usual; after which you add the same quantity of urine and at the expiration of five or six days, two drachms of arsenic; it will then be fit for use.

*Madder*
The root of this European herb was used to create a variety of shades of red, from orange and russet, through pinks and light reds to muddier, brownish shades.

*Woad*
The leaves of this European herb from the mustard family were used extensively in Tudor times to create a blue dye. The process involved drying and crushing the leaves, and then composting them with manure. They were fermented for several weeks and produced such an appalling smell that Queen Elizabeth banned the production of woad within 5 miles of any royal estate!

*Weld*
This plant was used to create a variety of shades of yellow. This biennial plant was also called Dyer's Rocket, Dyer's Broom and Dyer's Mignonette.

Colours and brightness determined the value of dyes. The poorer people wore clothes in shades of yellow, russet, green, pale blues and pinks. Fabric was also dyed by adding other botanical and natural materials to the heated mixtures, such as moss, walnut, oak galls and rust. The higher classes wore more vibrant and darker, more intense hues, made from expensive imported dyes, and these strong colours bestowed status on the wearers. Expensive dyes were created from natural materials, just like cheaper dyes, but from some exotic sources!

## Tyrian Purple

This dye was made from the shells of the *Mediterranean Murex*, in Tyre (The Lebanon) – and since Roman times was associated with rulers and Emperors, when it took an astonishing (and not environmentally friendly!) 10,000 murex to dye cloth for one toga. This rich, velvety deep purple was by the time of Elizabeth I quite literally worth its weight in gold and was even more sought after for its status. The production of Tyrian Purple had virtually ceased by the time Elizabeth was 20 years old after the fall of Constantinople in 1453.

## Crimson and Scarlet

Expensive and much sought after crimson and scarlet dyes were both produced from the bodies of insects – a strange concept perhaps to modern palates, and yet I can still remember a pot of cochineal in my mother's pantry; to be fair, I am in my fifties!

Cochineal had been produced since the time of the Aztecs in Central America and was brought back to Europe by Spanish Conquistadores. Pre-Columbian peoples had domesticated the beetle and farmed it to produce colour for over 2,000 years before the Spanish invaders 'discovered' it and brought it back to Europe. This tiny beetle, *Dactylopius Coccus* was the source of the rich red that became much beloved by the Elizabethans. The unfortunate beetle lived on prickly pear cactus before being collected, crushed, boiled and dried. Spain held the monopoly for cochineal at this time. The beetles yielded a strong, bright red that was around ten times more powerful than the red dyes previously available. Art historian Elena Phipps talks about the versatility of cochineal dye:

> To make cochineal red, the colorant (mainly carminic acid) is extracted from the dried bodies of the female insects in water. A mordant, or mineral salt, often alum (aluminum sulphate), is required to help bond the dye to the fibres. Other additives such as acids and alkali have traditionally been used to shift the naturally bright pink hue of cochineal to deep crimson, purple, or black.

She went on, in her work *Cochineal Red: The Art History of a Color* published in *The Metropolitan Museum of Art Bulletin* to emphasise the importance of cochineal to the Spanish crown:

> Cochineal, along with gold and silver from the Americas, enabled the Spanish Crown to finance its empire [...] while establishing its global monopoly and dominance of sea trade.

Cochineal was soon sought after all over Europe. Britain's soldiers were even clad in scarlet beetle-dyed wool coats when they went into battle; hence the name 'Redcoats'.

Before cochineal, kermes was a source of red dye. It was also produced from the bodies of insects; this time, a Mediterranean insect. Female insects *Kermes Vermilio Planchon* and *Kermes Ilicis* were found on the small evergreen tree the Kermes Oak, in southern Europe. It dated back to the ancients in Egypt and Rome. The dye was produced by drying the bodies and fermenting them in liquid. It is interesting to note that the words *crimson* in English and *carmoisine* in French are both derived from *kermes* – a humble insect.

*Indigo Blue*

Indigo was derived from plants (*Indigofera Tinctoria*) from India. This imported plant created a rich, deep blue colour much stronger than that provided by woad. The dye was produced by fermentation and subsequent filtering, and then it was dried and pressed into cakes of dye.

*Saffron Yellow*

Rich saffron yellow dye was produced from the vivid red stigma and stamens at the centre of the lovely but unassuming saffron crocus (*Crocus Sativus*). The brightest colour is produced by boiling the stigma (a female part of the flower), but colour is also produced by treating the stamen (a male part of the flower that produces pollen). Saffron was imported from Spain, Greece and the Orient.

On display at Hampton Court Palace is a piece of fabric dating back to the reign of Queen Elizabeth I. The Bacton Altar Cloth as it is known is displayed in a T-shape and although faded by time and light, is highly decorated and very interesting from a dyes point of view as it still shows elements of the reds and blues that the fabric contained.

This altar cloth has been brought to the palace for display as it is now thought to be an altered dress that once belonged to Queen Elizabeth herself. The decoration is embroidered directly onto the fabric itself rather than appliqued which was the more common practice for something as highly decorative. Both this and the fact that the fabric itself is cloth of silver, the use of which was restricted at the time, suggest that this dress may have been part of the queen's wardrobe.

The blues within the cloth have been shown to be indigo imported from India rather than woad or a more domestically available choice and the red has been traced as cochineal that originated in Mexico. The fact that the dyes were imported in this manner adds weight to the idea of the altar cloth originally being a royal garment as it adds to the likely already high cost that a dress of this type would have demanded. The side that is displayed has been washed out by the light in the time it had been displayed in St Faith's church in Bacton, however, the back of the cloth is still said to display a brighter and more preserved set of colours. The piece is a good example of the way in which dyes can fade over time but also shows us that even when exposed to light, natural dyes can still show through even after hundreds of years.

By the early 1500s, Germany, France and Holland had begun the cultivation of dye plants as an industry, and much of these 'foreign' dyestuffs were imported to England. The import of these 'unnecessary foreign wares' to England led in part to the Sumptuary Laws created in the reign of Elizabeth I.

Sumptuary Laws were nothing new. These laws had been imposed by monarchs to curb the expenditure of some people in society. The rich merchant classes that began to emerge in the Medieval period grew massively with the Tudor expansion in trade. The crown sought to limit the types of food, furniture, and clothing that people could buy, even if they had the wealth. These controls supported the class system and kept rich merchants from less than noble backgrounds from 'passing' in society as their 'betters'.

In the Elizabethan era, these Sumptuary Laws were very strict about clothing – right down to the colours. Colours held meaning at the time. They gave out signals about the person wearing the clothes. Purple clothes were still reserved for the nobility. Violet, indigo, gold, silver, crimson and scarlet were the province of the nobility. Lower classes of women, for example, were only permitted to wear clothing in brown, yellow, beige, green, russet, orange, grey and woad blue. The laws were strictly enforced. Anyone wearing colours they were not entitled to wear under the Statutes of Apparel enacted in 1574 were punished in draconian ways. Fines, confiscation of property and even execution were punishments meted out to offenders. It is an amazing thought in the modern era to think that even colours were legislated against to keep the poor in their place!

In certain places, dyeing as an occupation was a major source of employment. Many dyers on a commercial scale had small to medium businesses but some were on a grander scale such as Jack of Newbury, who in the sixteenth century employed forty dyers and used half a ton of woad every week!

By the Stuart era, dyeing was a highly specialised industry. Many materials remained popular from previous periods such as woad, madder, indigo, weld, galls, and cochineal, but there were new materials beginning to arrive in Europe as a result of the trade with the New World and other markets.

Brasil and redwood had been known since the middle ages (and is even mentioned in Chaucer's *The Nun's Priest's Tale*) but came into its own in the Stuart era. When South America was invaded and colonised, the red dye from the *Caesalpinia echinata* or redwood became a popular source of red dye.

In 1672, Privy Council records show that a petition was raised against the importation of sanders, a type of red sandalwood from India. The petition states that it was 'a very fading cheeting dye.' One has to wonder if this petition was truly about the quality of the dye or more an attempt to put a halt to its import for commercial and financial reasons.

Logwood has an interesting story. It was banned in 1581 and this was not repealed until 1673. It was suggested that the reason for this repeal was because dyers in England now knew how to fix the colours correctly; however, it seems more likely that England now had logwood plantations of its own and did not have to rely upon Spanish imports.

Another dye material introduced from the Americas was a type of fustic, which makes yellow shades. Venetian Sumach was already available; *Cladrastis Tinctoria* also became available.

In terms of mordants, up until the sixteenth century alum had to be imported to Britain. At the beginning of the seventeenth century dyers were able to access alum from alum shale. By 1635, 1,800 tons a year were being extracted in Whitby – making Britain self-sufficient in terms of supply.

So, this period was a time of huge development in terms of dyeing, with the wealth of materials available growing year by year as traders travelled to new regions of the world. Technological and scientific developments were also continuing apace during this period and these inventions and discoveries (such as alum extraction) all helped to drive the dye industry forward at a fast pace.

*Chapter 5*

# Georgian and Regency Era Traditional Dyeing

Textile 'finishing' was a massive trade in Georgian times. Finishing was the term used to describe what happened after yarn and cloth was created, and encompassed bleaching, dyeing and printing. As yarn and fabric production increased exponentially at this time due to mechanisation, a bottleneck was created where a log-jam of fabric and yarn sat waiting to be finished. The invention of the water wheel and the introduction of steam power led to developments in the finishing industry, where chemical bleaching and steam-powered dyeing and printing sped up the process for the hungry factories waiting to turn fabric and yarn into apparel and furnishings. At least sixty-seven finishing works were established in the Manchester area alone in the eighteenth century. Water and steam drove the great machinery, and in 1825 the Buckton Vale Bleaching and Print Works was established. By the end of the nineteenth century it had become the largest bleaching, dyeing and printing works in the North West. The Kirklees Valley was also rich in finishing sites, with an astonishing twelve competing businesses sited along a 4 kilometre stretch of the valley. These factories mainly bleached and dyed cotton cloth, but there were also print works in the area.

Dyeing underwent huge changes in the Georgian era, as discoveries came thick and fast around the world. Jeremias Friedrich Gülich, a dyer born in 1733 in Cannstatt, Germany published his book *Die rechte und wahrhafte Färbe-Kunst* or *The Right and True Colouring Art* in 1751. This book brought together multiple ways in which wools, silks and linens could be dyed. He then followed this by publishing *Vollständiges Färbe und Bleichbuch* or Complete Dye and Bleach Book in 1779. This major work, split across six volumes was filled with technical knowledge on the processes of dyeing available within the eighteenth century.

Gülich's knowledge and passion for dyeing eventually led him to purchasing a cotton mill in 1785, which was solely responsible for supplying the German army with clothing. Gülich's methods of dyeing, especially those used for sheep's wool were taken as the standard for the industry at the time.

Although the two men never met, Jeremias was recognised for his work in Johann Wolfgang von Goethe's 1810 book *Theory of Colours*. Goethe describes the wide range of knowledge possessed by Gülich as well as suggesting he feels the man should have been lauded and should be more widely known.

In 1743 Johann Christian Barth, a lawyer from Grossenhain combined indigo with sulphuric acid, then rather picturesquely known as *oil of vitriol* to create *Indigo Carmine* more popularly known as *Saxon Blue* or *Prussian Blue*. The technique to create *Saxon Blue* became public knowledge in the latter half of the 1740s, and quickly spread as others sought ways to improve the initial technique. This new dye could be produced easily as the acid process meant that less heat was needed than in other dyeing processes and the process was quicker overall. Certain disadvantages such as its relatively poor wash fastness and ability to fade were initially overlooked and the dye quickly became popular.

Despite this early popularity, the drawbacks of the fading colour and the inability to wash fabric dyed in this manner without the subsequent colour-run led to a waning interest over time. A more colour-fast and stable dye was needed.

Carl Scheele, a chemist from Sweden created a new dye colour, *Scheele's Green* in 1775. The colour had a significant advantage over the green dyes of the day. Dyers previously were only able to produce green dye by mixing yellow and blue dyes to achieve it. This labour-intensive process could produce beautiful colours, but all too often, however, the results would not last, and the colours would begin to wash out and fade.

Scheele's Green produced a one-step lasting colour of equal quality to those produced by more traditional, and more complex processes, making it a hugely attractive dyeing option. However, the colour was produced by combining arsenious oxide with a sodium carbonate solution and as such, the arsenic present in the colouring made the colour toxic. Bad news for dyers – and people wearing clothes made from fabric dyed with this vivid colour. By the 1780s printed cotton had reached its peak as a daywear fashion choice. This taste would change in the next decade, however, as the more classically-inspired gowns produced during the 1790s meant that the fabric was not as suitable given its stiffer texture. Dressmakers instead preferred to use thinner and more free-flowing fabric such as muslin for this new style of dress.

As with all fashion trends, printed cottons would rise in popularity again as more complex patterns and garments became increasingly popular in the early decades of the nineteenth century. In the same way as today, these changes in favour of fabric and style would not have been as evident everywhere at once. While the Georgian court and the chic ladies of the cities would have adapted quickly, more rural areas of the country would have taken longer to adopt new fashions. In some cases the more flowing style of clothing would have been impractical, as the more hardwearing cotton fabrics would have been more suited to working situations and could be easily washed without damage.

The Wilhelm Dye and White Lead Company, based in Schweinfurt in Germany, completed development of a new kind of green dye in 1814. The dye was known as *Emerald Green* due to its bright qualities. Like Scheele's Green, Emerald Green was produced using arsenic, and so naturally was toxic both for the producers and consumers of products coloured with the dye. This didn't affect its popularity, sadly. Vanity came before safety – a problem that persists to the modern day. The colour was introduced at a time in which changes in lighting technology (namely a change from gaslit sources as opposed to the more muted lighting produced by candles) were making bright colours pop at a party in a way they never had before. This led to the muted colours of some dyes of the time seeming drab, and ladies wanted to stand out as the belle of the ball in the new, glittering lights. Sadly, their love of vivid green made them more likely moths to the flame who would fade and die. It wasn't long before the colour made is transition from clothing to home décor, being used to colour wallpaper and floor coverings – so danger was everywhere.

If you have watched the television series *Bridgerton*, you may be interested in colour and dye in the Regency period. As always, bright and strong colours were the most expensive. Either the dye itself was expensive due to import and production costs (such as cochineal) or because it took several dips to make the colour dark, or overdyeing was needed to create a bright colour.

Block printing had made printed fabric expensive until the end of the eighteenth century, but with the development of roller printing the delightful flower-sprigged fabrics beloved of the Regency ladies (and dandies!) became more widely available – even down to the working classes. As brightly-dyed fabrics became more easily available, fashions dictated 'this season's colour' and ladies could modishly follow the trends. An interesting side note to all of this colour (and the way garments were made from layers of different fabrics) is that outer clothes in particular were not able to be laundered. They were sponged, steamed, brushed and treated with hot sand and Fuller's earth to remove grease stains. Eventually they would look tired and grubby. These clothes were sent to the dyer who could re-dye the garment to make it look like new. We could learn a lot in the modern era from this commitment to reuse and recycle chic!

## Chapter 6

# Victorian Traditional Dyeing

F rom the 1850s onwards, the use of often expensive, often gentler natural dyes was declining as new, brighter and cheaper synthetic colours were being created.

Growing great swathes of dyestuff and importing expensive exotic botanicals was being replaced. The textile industry was burgeoning. The demand for dyes was growing rapidly and they needed to be both cost effective and easy to manage. With the rise of industrialisation, the study of coal and tar by chemists would lead to a boom in the creation of synthetic dyes. German chemist August Wilhelm Von Hofmann was the director of the Royal College of Chemistry in England. He lectured, trained and mentored a great many of the chemists who would grow to be giants in the English dye industry.

One of his pupils, a Londoner called William H. Perkin, created mauve – the first synthetic dye – in 1856. He actually created this lovely colour by accident. He was attempting to synthesize artificial quinine, an important anti-malarial drug for Victorian-era travellers and settlers in the colonies. As Perkin worked away over his Easter break in his home laboratory, he used coal tar as a source of aniline. When he oxidised it with potassium dichromate he produced a rather sticky black syrupy material that seemed like a failure. However, when he came to clean up after himself (as all good scientists should) he flushed out a flask with ethanol. This clean up produced a vivid purple solution – and made history! Perkin had created the first synthetic dye. Previously, vivid purple had only been worn by the richest citizens such as royalty and high clergy as it had been made from large numbers of *Mediterranean Murex* molluscs. Now, at last, purple was available to ordinary citizens. This colour was at first known as aniline purple, and subsequently *mauveine*. Perkin's family encouraged the young chemist to try to dye samples of cloth and lovely results were obtained. He sent a sample to Pullars of Perth, a dye works, who tested the sample and approved it as a commercially viable dye, and Perkins patented his production method. With funds from his father, Perkins set up a factory in partnership with his brother, mass producing the purple dye. He toured the country giving lectures on his discovery, including an audience with the Royal Society in 1859. The colour gained so much fame that it made its way into the Oxford English Dictionary in the same year. It even made it into the publication *All the Year Round*, a weekly journal conducted by Charles Dickens. The purple dye was described thus:

> It is rich and pure, and fit for anything; be it fan, slipper, gown, ribbon, handkerchief, tie, or glove. It will lend lustre to the soft changeless twilight of ladies' eyes – it will take any shape to find an excuse to flutter round her cheek – to cling (as the wind blows it) up to her lips – to kiss her foot – to whisper at her ear. O Perkins's [sic] purple, thou art a lucky and a favoured colour!

The colour was wildly popular. Empress Eugenie, Napoleon III's consort wore Perkin's purple and made it fashionable in upper echelons of society – and this of course filtered down through the classes in society. Queen Victoria sealed societal approval for purple hues when she attended her eldest daughter's grand wedding wearing a gown of delicate mauve. The gown may be seen in the painting *The Marriage of Victoria, Princess Royal* painted by artist John Phillip. The colour was soon a royal favourite, and Victoria wore it regularly when in mourning for her husband Albert.

Between 1881 and 1901, even British 'Penny Lilac' postage stamps were a lovely shade of mauve.

Further research showed that coal tar would give other dyes. By 1900, more than fifty compounds had been synthesized using coal tar. Internationally, chemists raced to produce other synthetic dyes from coal tar. Their main method was to study the structure of natural dyestuff and then subsequently to develop a similar synthetic dye in the lab. These could then be manufactured on a grand scale. Developments in science and technology were driving industry – an exciting development that made many industrialists salivate at the dreamed-of riches these new dyes would bring. In 1868, scientists discovered that alizarin, a natural dye, could be synthesized from coal tar. In June 1869 both Perkin and BASF, a German dye company, filed patents for the process within days of one another. Natural alizarin producers were swiftly pushed out of business by this cheap alternative. Perkin's works was producing over 400 tonnes of synthetic alizarin a year – at a quarter of the price of the natural dye.

A similar, if drawn-out story can be told about the natural indigo industry. Baeyer synthesized indigo in 1880, but it was only when BASF invested £2 million that a commercially viable synthetic indigo was created seventeen years later. The natural indigo industry struggled on for a few years but then largely petered out. Natural dyes would enjoy a brief resurgence during the First World War, due to changes in factory usage and supply chains, but once again fell neglected immediately post war.

In an interesting aside, when German doctor Paul Ehrlich was trying to find an antiseptic substance that could be used to treat bacterial infections (remember, this was before commercial antibiotics were developed by Alexander Fleming, professor of bacteriology at St Mary's Hospital, London in 1928) he found that one of the stains he used to prepare microscope slides actually *killed* bacteria. This yellow dye, called *flavine* was subsequently used to kill the microbes responsible for infecting wounds to create abscesses. Lots of other innovative drugs were developed from coal tar – so it could be said that they owe their origins to the Victorian dye industry!

Dyes in the Victorian era continued to be an often deadly affair. Scheele's Green was still causing horrible reactions and even deaths – from blistered hands and skin exposed to the dyed fabric, to deaths from poisoning. Babies were reported as dying after playing on arsenic-dyed rugs, and people were even poisoned by green wallpaper! Vomiting, high blood pressure, delirium, shock and convulsions were a high price to pay for vivid green hues. There were even rumours (according to Victoria Finlay in *Color: A Natural History of the Palette*) that Napoleon died not as a result of stomach cancer, but as a result of the green dye in the wall décor at Longwood House in St Helena where he died.

A visiting foreign dignitary told Queen Victoria that her wallpaper made him ill. Far from a comment on her taste (or lack of it) with its mousy smell this toxic green dye did make people feel very ill indeed, and Victoria had the wallpaper removed.

Doctors were aware of this widespread problem. William Hinds, a doctor based in Birmingham wrote about the dreadful poisoning cases he was seeing as a result of arsenic in wallpaper and home furnishings in 1857. He said, 'A great deal of slow poisoning is going on in Great Britain.'

Newspapers ran articles about the dangers, and there were cartoons of death as a skeleton, lurking in richly-furnished homes. Lucinda Hawksley describes these deadly dyed wallpapers in detail in her fascinating book, *Bitten by Witch Fever: Wallpaper & Arsenic in the Nineteenth Century Home*. Hawksley details 275 gorgeous wallpapers which were tested by the British National Archives – and all were found to contain arsenic. By 1874, Britain was producing an amazing 32,000,000 rolls of brightly-coloured – and often deadly – wallpaper, heavily coloured and suitable for the Victorian taste for ornate decorations. The ridiculous thing is, Victorians knew that arsenic was poisonous (they used it routinely for killing vermin such as rats and mice, and even jokingly called it 'inheritance powder' when it was used to commit murder!) yet they still plastered their homes in materials dyed using this toxic chemical. But then again, arsenic was to be found at the time in cosmetics and even paint on toys.

Denial was the order of the day. People joked that they would be safe as long as they didn't lick the wallpaper – sadly not true. Others insisted doctors were lying.

Workers in the factories that produced the dyed materials were in danger every day. Factory conditions were famously appalling at the time, but in the case of the girls working in the factories producing dyed goods, their work was killing them on a daily basis – in the most dreadful ways. In 1861, a terrible case involving a young woman named Matilda Scheurer came to light. Matilda worked in a factory applying arsenic green dye to the popular fabric flowers that adorned the hats and décolletage of Victorian high fashion. The poor girl vomited green foamy fluid, and the whites of her eyes were a vivid shade of green. Just before she died, she said that everything she saw was tinted a green colour. Investigations into factory conditions found that many women worked in the same awful conditions and often had sores that wept as a result of the poisonous dye.

It took until 1895 for regulations to change working conditions in factories to ensure at least a measure of safety for workers in the dye industry working with arsenic based dyes. By now however, its popularity had waned.

Arsenic was not the only danger to health. Artificial dyes were invented thick and fast, and the coal tar dyes of the 1840s and 1850s caused all manner of health issues. Aniline purple, for example, caused

'Mauve Measles' – a nasty rash which irritated and inflamed the skin. Workers were exposed to toxic chemicals such as naphtalidine, toluene, dinitrobenzene, aniline and naphthalene. Added to these dangers, once the dye baths were finished with as depleted, they were usually dumped in lakes and rivers, poisoning the environment and water courses. This of course had a knock-on effect on public health as water supplies were contaminated.

So, the dye industry boomed in Victorian England like many other textiles industries. The populace were hungry for colours and industry provided them across the commonwealth – but at a cost to the environment and the health of its workers.

## Chapter 7

# Twentieth-Century Traditional Dyeing

In 1901, a German chemist by the name of René Bohn, while attempting to create a synthetic alternative to indigo, discovered what would become known as Indanthrene dyes. These dyes were consistent and reliable, able to be washed without running and were not significantly degraded by light as some dyes could be. This dye and its success were of such high value to BASF, Bohn's employer at the time, that their hotel created in 1960 at their Ludwigshafen site for business guests and customers is still known as the Hotel René Bohn in honour of his contribution.

James Morton was born in Scotland in 1867 and became part of his father Alexander Morton's weaving company. It was with this company that he would start to work towards the creation of 'Fast Dyes' as he became dissatisfied with how quickly the colours used in the company's tapestries would fade after seeing examples of recently supplied, and vastly faded work his company had produced while visiting Liberty in London in 1904. He employed a chemist called John Christie Jnr, who was the son of John Christie of the United Turkey Red Company, in order to aid him in development of the new dyes.

Once they had achieved their aim of creating dyes that would stand the test of time, Morton was able to present tapestries using the new dyes to Liberty and prove their new lasting colour to the directors, having them displayed once again in the prestigious store front. Morton then turned his attention to a wider market, realising that Liberty would appeal only to those with a larger disposable income. In order to do this, Morton decided on the name 'Sundour' combining the word sun, the enemy of a dye's permanence and the word dour, which was colloquially used as the word for stubborn, playing on the dye's ability to resist the sun's effects. The dyes would go on to be a successful product, also being used by the likes of Burberry in their fashion ranges.

The downside of this staying power was that the range of colours that could be produced by Sundour was limited, as some colours were ultimately still not able to be created to the standard Morton felt he had set.

The First World War created a difficult situation for the American fashion industry. At the time war broke out across the globe, America imported a large percentage of its dye from German dye works. While America wouldn't enter the war during its first two years, the blockades set up by Britain's Royal Navy meant that supply routes were effectively cut off and so American clothing companies found themselves without the means to create many of the colourful garments they were producing.

The result of this was that the American textile manufacturers and fashion houses turned to a palette of black and white. This is because American organisations were still able to easily produce black dyes by using sulphur which would be reliably light and wash-fast when compared with their options in terms of producing colours from natural dyes.

When the United States introduced its 'trading with the enemy' Act in 1917, it allowed the American government to seize assets belonging to German nationals within the US. This happened to include plants owned by the Bayer Company among others which also gave them the use of their dyeing equipment and allowed them to use patents that belonged to those German companies registered in the United States. Over the next two years, the US government would invest significantly in the dye industry, totalling over $450,000,000 which allowed them to strengthen their national ability to produce and supply the domestic clothing industry as well as to begin exporting elsewhere.

Other countries were also working to build their own supply of dye products at this time, as Germany had not only been a major exporter to the United States but was responsible for around 80–90 per cent of the global dye export market.

This brings us back to James Morton who had, following his prior success, turned his attention to the production of a specific dye colour. Morton set out to create a green dye that had so far eluded the German dye producers he had worked with previously. After four years, Morton's company, now known as 'Scottish Dyes', produced 'Caledon Jade Green' in 1920. This vat dye was a great success for Morton's company and was found to equal the fastness of any dye he had produced before. Morton would eventually collaborate with René Bohn and BASF on the large-scale production of Caledon Jade Green showing that the British-made dye was taken seriously by the larger, more experienced German company. In 1956, Imperial Chemical Industries Ltd produced the first of their fibre reactive dyes known as Procion dyes. These dyes were able to bond directly to the fibres of the fabric they were applied to, which gave them a significant advantage over the other dye types being used at the time. One such advantage being that because of the process used to apply the reactive dyes it was unlikely that colour-run from a garment dyed in this manner would cause discolouration on another. This meant that it was safer than it had been previously to wash dyed clothing of different colours together without risking one item of clothing affecting the colour of another. Imperial Chemical would go on to introduce Procinyl dyes in 1959, adapting their existing technology to dye nylon which by this point was a well-established and very popular material within the clothing industry. Procion dye's ability to keep colours separated would become valuable for a specific type of dyeing also. The technique of tie-dyeing was perfect for Procion dyes and their particular bonded application to fabric and indeed are still recommended highly when using this technique today.

Tie-dye can trace its origins much further back than the 1960s with examples of it found in Japanese 'Shibori' style, 'Kanoko Shibori', and Indian 'Bandhani' with examples found dated from 4,000 BC. The Nigerian 'Adire' technique which, while certainly being used in the early part of the twentieth century, has also been suggested to have existed as far back as the eleventh century. It cannot be denied, however, that its popularity in the western world exploded in 1960s America, being adopted as a fashion choice of the counterculture championed by musicians involved in the psychedelia sound and by protestors against the war in Vietnam choosing tie-dye shirts as their de facto uniform. Despite tie-dye becoming a symbol of the counterculture, there were those who saw opportunity. Don Price, a marketer at RIT dyes realised the effect that Woodstock would have and had hundreds of tie-dye shirts created using RIT dyes to sell at the festival. The gamble worked and RIT became a *go to* brand for those creating tie-dye fashion at the time. This association helped to turn around the company's finances and RIT dyes are still producing a range of colours now.

So twentieth-century dyeing methods developed quickly as technology advanced, and more chemicals were created to make dyes fast, and non-fading. This development would continue to flourish as we moved into the twenty-first century.

*Chapter 8*

# Modern Dyeing

D ue to significant technological advancements in the last century, commercially available dyes are now easily accessible and come in a range of colours that producers like Bohn and Morton could only have dreamed of. Companies such as Dylon, Abbey Color and Avocet create a range of colours for home and industrial use able to be applied to a wide range of fabrics. However, despite this mass availability of dyes that some would view as convenient, the recent past has seen a resurgence of interest in the field of natural dyeing. Artisans the world over are working with traditional techniques to create authentic dyes from plants and natural sources to be used in a range of textile arts and fashions. Substances like woad, madder, nettle, onion skin and a range of tree barks and mosses have returned to use to create a dye palette that while never left behind, had been supplanted in most cases by the variety made possible with synthetic dyes. These natural dyes also have the benefit of usually being more environmentally friendly than some of the mass produced dyes made today and certainly more so than those produced during the early years of the twentieth century. A lot of these artisanal textile workers and artists are also turning their hand to teaching, in order to pass on the skills and traditions they have learned, helping to ensure that the ability to produce a range of hues from plants that may well be in your garden now are not lost.

Part of the resurgence of natural dyeing on such a wide scale could be attributed to the modern wave of online shopping and the wave of resource and information that can bring. A brief search through most online marketplaces will result in a much wider range of supplies being available than you might be able to find locally. Items such as dye kits for specialist colourings like indigo using natural ingredients, individual colour powders, seeds for woad, madder, weld and individually dyed yarns and wools to be used in textile artwork. The last two items being particularly important for farm diversification and finding alternative sources of income for farmers of rare breed sheep, goats and alpaca. Information can be sourced in the same manner, meaning you don't need to be living near an expert in order to heed their advice and it's easier than it was to find specialist books than ever before. Books detailing information on creating dyes, planting a dye garden, how to gain a wide variety of colours and the history of dyeing can all be found with the correct searches. Open access to these online markets has also increased exposure for small businesses, artisans, textile artists and creators of small-batch natural dyes. Video content hosting sites can be used in a similar manner with a lot of the producers taking advantage of this new exposure by becoming content creators. This allows them to provide instructional videos on which plants to select for which colours, how to apply them, what mordants will be the most effective and which products will work with which fabrics. This increase in online presence also means that those looking for fashions that might use more natural colours rather than the brighter synthetic colours found on the high street are able to access them directly from the people making them.

Over time the industrial scale of dye production has naturally started to take its toll, both on the environment as we've discussed but also on the health of workers and the communities that surround the dyeworks. India has always been connected to indigo, however, the large amount of waste water produced by its indigo factories has been said to have poor health implications for those living near them as they have begun to make the water supplies toxic. However, this problem doesn't just affect India, in fact, India is only the third largest exporter of textiles, the second being the combined member states of the European Union and the first being China. Reports of water contamination and poor health caused by the toxic and carcinogenic chemicals, such as formaldehyde, that can be used in order to meet global demand for 'fast fashion' are easy to find yet hard to reconcile with the public image of the industry. There are those within the industry that are attempting to find ways to reduce things like wastewater in order to negate the effects that the industry is having on the environment, producers and consumers alike. Colorifix is one such example. The company exists to create a naturally-inspired solution that will allow the dyeing industry to use a lot less water and to remove the usage of so many of the harmful chemicals that can be involved in large-scale textile dyeing. They aim to do this via bioengineering micro organisms to replicate natural colouration, meaning that synthetic dye on a large scale is still possible, with less variance than natural methods might result in, while still reducing pollution and allowing industry to continue. It should be noted, however, that it's not just elements outside of the dyeing industry looking to make a difference either. Adidas, a long-running name in the fashion and sportswear industry have invested in using a pressurized carbon dioxide process they call 'DryDye' which negates their need for water usage in the dye process. While this obviously means a lot less waste water, it still uses chemicals which organisations are looking to reduce. Although the indigo dye industry still uses a natural base for some of its colouration, it can often be the chemical used as a mordant needed to bring the colour fastness up to standard that can be the harmful element. As a result of this there are organisations who are currently conducting research into the creation of safer and non-toxic mordants that could be used on a wide scale. This naturally would help to decrease the harmful effects that the industry at large can cause.

So the modern era of dyeing has its eyes firmly on the development of eco-friendly dyes, due both to legislative controls on pollution and to the rise in interest of consumers in green solutions. Whilst commercial dyers wrestle with these issues, there is burgeoning interest in artisanal circles in particular in the use of natural dyestuffs.

*Chapter 9*

# Artisan Interviews

The best way to find out about the modern artisans working in traditional dyeing today is to ask them about their experiences, inspirations and artistic practices. With the advent of the Internet, it is thankfully easier than ever to find a window into the creative world of these artisans, and to find out more. A quick search on websites such as Etsy, Folksy, Instagram and Pinterest takes the seeker down a glorious rabbit hole of colour and explores a world of seemingly arcane, apothecary-level art making and experiences that will thrill even the most jaded of crafting hearts.

These artists and crafters earn a living with their art and crafts. Many of them have taken the leap into self-employment, and sustain themselves and their families with their skill and artistry. I asked these artists a series of questions, and encouraged them to describe their motivations, inspirations and goals for the future. It is a fascinating window into a highly creative, innovative and experimental world. They have taken traditional techniques and allowed them to evolve as they have explored their own ways of working.

You can find out more about each artist by following the links provided for their websites and social media. Many of these artisans supply tools, seeds, dyes and equipment to support the nascent dyer. You can buy their products directly, or even commission dyed pieces yourself, and help to support the hand-made industry directly at source!

## Pauline Campbell

I'm 52 years old, and married to my biggest supporter. I have two beautiful grandchildren whom I hope to pass on my craft to. I live for my craft and have a craft room in my home, where I will spend hours, either taking pics, sorting through my stash to get inspiration or doing paper crafts. No craft is safe and I like to dip in and out of lots of different mediums.

*What first attracted you to your craft?*
I have always loved knitting and crochet, but after joining Instagram it really took on a different level, and I loved knitting socks as it allowed me to try all the lovely indie yarn out there, which led to me dyeing my own. With crochet I wanted to try something different than crocheting my usual blankets, although I do still love making blankets too.

*Can you describe your journey into your craft? How did you get started? For example, do you have particular training or qualifications, or are you self-taught?*
My nanny first introduced me to knitting when she was knitting her famous Aran cardigans and Icelandic jumpers for all the family, to keep us warm in the Scottish winters. She bought me my first ball of wool, and about forty-four years later I'm still loving it. Most of my knitting and crochet is self-taught, and has evolved slowly but gradually to delving deeper into fibre arts. Crochet came about ten years after I learned to knit.

*Do you have any inspirations or influences? This could include particular artisans, periods in history etc.*
I love anything from the Victorian Era, especially the Industrial Age, I also love the sub-culture of Steampunk, which has flavours of an alternative Victorian style. I also take inspiration from the seasons, especially autumn, and the warm tones that feature a lot in my yarn dyeing.

*What do you enjoy most about working with the materials that you choose to work with?*

I love the process of dyeing as each batch I make is unique. Before I dye them I choose the name for them after a theme based on Victoriana, once they are dyed, dried and twisted, I then attach a story to them, so that when people are knitting with the yarn, they are taken on a journey through the different tones and shades

*Please describe the tools of your craft, and how you use them.*

For the dyeing, I use citric acid, which helps the fibres to absorb the wool dye, I also use flat aluminium pans to simmer the yarn, and another method I use is to steam the yarn. With the crochet I use metal hooks and 100 per cent cotton yarn, as I feel this gives a better structure to my amigurumi. I am most proud of designing some of my crochet dolls, which at the moment I am developing patterns for my Etsy shop.

*Describe your business. What items do you make? Do you sell items – if so, what? Do you teach courses? Describe the thing you have made that has made you most proud.*

I have an Etsy shop that I use to sell my hand dyed yarn. It is a fairly new project for me so I am still developing it and hope to have a website eventually. I also intend to start selling PDF patterns for my amigurumi.

*Please describe a typical day – as if an artist has one!*

I work outside the industry four days a week, but after work I typically come home and aim to be settling down each night crocheting or developing amigurumi patterns. On my days off I batch dye yarn, and create colourways to reflect my themes.

*What traditional 'heritage' methods do you use in your craft?*
I incorporate the traditional craft of Needle Felting into my amigurumi, by using this method to make more realistic eyes, and also hairstyles.

*How have you adapted heritage or historic methods for the modern day?*
Traditionally crochet thread would be used for doilies and filet work etc., but I use lots of different weights of threads to make outfits and accessories for my amigurumi.

*What advice would you give someone starting out in your field?*
If I were to give advice it would be to try lots of different fibre arts and see which ones suit your time/environment best. I have tried lots of different crafts, and have finally found my niche!

I also love amateur photography, and when taking pics of my yarn for sale, I always try to set the picture up to bring the yarn to life, I also love digital crafting (though basic) – and I make all my own labels, tags, and stitch markers. I even have a full-leg tattoo that includes balls of wool, and Victorian steampunk images, and my favourite is a steampunk bird pulling a strand of wool from a ball, and it spells out 'Nanny' – representing my beautiful gran who started my love of all things yarn.

I am an active member on Instagram as (Knitonecrochetone), Etsy as (SteampunkSheepYarns.Etsy.com/) and Facebook which I have just recently started using as SteampunkSheepYarns.

## Helen Melvin
*What first attracted you to your craft?*
I first started spinning in the early 1990s and about three years later I went to a natural dyeing workshop run by Clwyd Guild of Weavers Spinners and Dyers. I found both the colours and their complexity intensely satisfying and after this I started dyeing immediately and soon

bought my first book, Jill Goodwin's *A Dyer's Manual*, rapidly followed by Trudy Von Stralen's *Indigo Madder and Marigold*, and Jenny Dean's *Wild Colour*.

*Can you describe your journey into your craft? How did you get started? For example, do you have particular training or qualifications, or are you self-taught?*
I only went to a few workshops, one with Jenny Dean, and later on one about using concentrated extracts of natural dyes with Michele Wipplinger of EarthHues at Colour Congress in Iowa in the USA. I must mention J.N. Liles' *The Art and Craft of Natural Dyeing*, an extremely important book, which amongst other things taught me the importance of scouring and proper preparation. I also used his chapter on indigo to dye with different types of indigo vats to learn more of this complex subject, which proved to be the foundation of my indigo dyeing practice. At Colour Congress in the USA, I studied one day of a two-day workshop on using natural dyes as paints. I came back to the UK and spent a few years playing around with the technique before developing a range of natural dye inks based on medieval calligraphy inks. Now I have eighteen different colours all of my own recipes and available from my website. They are designed by me to be used for painting on paper but they can also with care be used for painting onto fabrics. I also sell them to many other artists.

In 2005 I put together a booklet of my natural dyeing notes ready for the very first Woolfest and this later became my first book on natural dyeing *Colours of the Earth*. This was to be followed over the next few years by a book on indigo dyeing *The Colours of the Sea & Sky*, Eco Dyeing *Colours of the World*, and on concentrated extracts *Colours of the Rainbow*. These are all regularly updated and still have their hand-painted covers available from my website. *(NB Author note: meeting Helen at Woolfest and buying her books was what initiated my own interest in natural dyeing some years ago. She is knowledgeable and generous with her expertise.)*

In 2007 I started experimenting with solar dyeing in Kilner jars, and allow the dyes to dye in the gentle heat of the sun over many months. I soon began to experiment with multi-coloured dyeing and now sell kits for other people to enjoy this fun way of dyeing too. I frequently have thirty or so pots on shelves outside my summer house.

*What traditional 'heritage' methods do you use in your craft?*
I make a dye called Saxon Blue. This is a seventeenth-century recipe which involves dissolving indigo in concentrated sulphuric acid. Please be aware though that J.N. Liles, who wrote the original recipe, has very poor health and many safety recommendations. Dressed up in protective clothing to make a batch of Saxon Blue I resemble a small plump Darth Vader, but it does make a fabulous turquoise blue, overdyed in cochineal, fustic and dyer's chamomile a glorious range of purples and greens can be made. I sell Saxon Blue in two sizes from my website and it's one of my most popular products and at times I struggle to keep pace with demand.

*How have you adapted heritage or historic methods for the modern day?*
I have a dye garden with many plants including the best ones for yellows, dyer's greenweed and weld. My good friend Enys Davies grows the dye plants for me and it is from her garden that we harvest kilos of dyer's chamomile. I sell all these dyes carefully dried and Eco-packaged.

## Mia Malone
My name is Mia Malone, I'm a lover of the great outdoors, a treasure seeker and a perpetual student. You will find me always looking for natural treasures wherever I go and my passion for learning means that I can often be found discovering new skills to turn my hand to. I'm also a wife and mother to the most amazing humans you could wish to meet.

Blush by Mia Malone.

Cherished Moments by Mia Malone.

Misty Morning by Mia Malone.

Seedlings by Mia Malone.

*Above left*: Stormy Seas by Mia Malone.

*Above right*: Gorgeous colour mix in this hand dyed fabric from Claire Phillips.

*Right*: Dyed fibres from Claire Phillips.

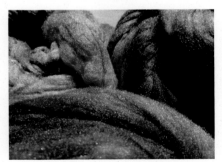

*Above left*: Small plant dyed hand woven bag by Eve Studd.

*Above right*: Fabric blankets, sometimes used in the process but the colours on these will most likely fade. They are objects of transient beauty which seems to reflect a quality of nature.

Plant dyed peg loomed hangings in progress, inspired by the Northumberland hills.

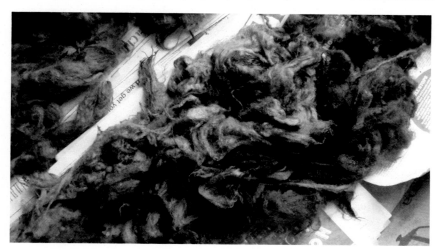

'Creating shades of green isn't as straightforward as some folk might expect, but the unpredictable variations make it my favourite dyeing work.' (Eve Studd)

Glorious landscape colours woven into a wallhanging.

Beautiful blues creating waves on fabric like a stormy sea.

*Above left*: Deep blue dyes with striking tones.

*Above right, below left and below right*: Hand dyed yarn from Karen Walthinsen.

*Above and left*: Beautiful botanicals and dye plants grown by Eve Studd, waiting to be processed.

Eco dyed piece from Eve Studd.

Karen Walthinsen's beautiful shawl.

Watching flowers change in warm water.

Sørlandskofte,
a traditional
pattern from
Southern
Norway
with Karen's
hand-dyed yarn.

Karen Walthinsen's delicate colours.

Variegated, naturally dyed skeins by
Karen Walthinsen.

Suzanne Dekel, artisanal dyer.

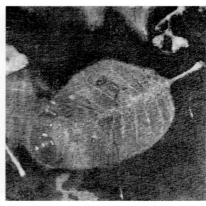

Suzanne Dekel's detailed eco printed materials.

Suzanne Dekel's gorgeous eco printed fabric.

Suzanne Dekel's yellow shades.

Suzanne Dekel's beautifully dyed fabric.

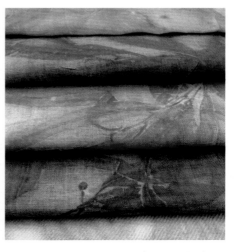

Suzanne Dekel's complementary shades.

*Above left*: Linda Illuminardi, artisanal dyer.

*Above right*: A selection of Linda Illuminardi's handmade eco printed books.

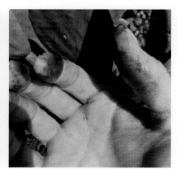

*Right*: Linda Illuminardi harvesting cochineal.

*Above left and above right*: Linda Illuminardi's eco dyeing.

*Right*: The finished product.

Linda Illuminardi's eco dyeing bundles.

Beautiful eco dyed felt from Linda Illuminardi.

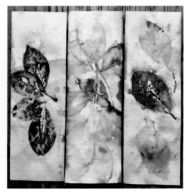

Eco dyed artwork from Linda Illuminardi.

Eco dyed paper from Linda Illuminardi.

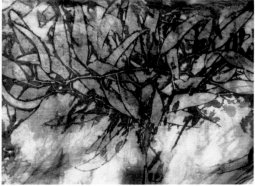

Bundles of promise – eco dyeing from Linda Illuminardi waiting to be unwrapped.

Beautiful eco dyeing by Linda Illuminardi.

My husband and our little girl have supported me through returning to university, setting up and running my business, as well as joining me with a love of nature and treasure hunting, it is with them that I find my peace and balance in life.

*What first attracted you to your craft?*
I have always had a fascination with nature after spending cherished moments with my grandad in the garden while he planted new shrubs and showed me which plants would attract bees and butterflies. I'm always reminded of these memories when I see floral fabrics or artwork and I think I have always wanted to find a craft that would allow me to harness those memories and create something inspired by my early connection with the great outdoors.

*Can you describe your journey into your craft? How did you get started? For example, do you have particular training or qualifications, or are you self-taught?*
I didn't find my passion for knitting and dyeing until I began my Foundation Degree in Fashion Design. I was asked to create knitted swatches during the first module and once I got the hang of it, well that was that, I taught myself complex stitch patterns and realised this was how I could create items inspired by nature.

I began hand dyeing fabrics and block printing when I couldn't find what I was looking for while creating my garment designs. My first block prints were of butterflies and I manipulated the fabric into folds to represent the wings of butterflies.

My connection to natural dyeing was fuelled as I wrote an essay reporting on the impact the fashion and textiles industry has on the environment. It was then that I realised as much as I wanted to work in the textiles industry, I wanted to preserve the environment not contribute to the crisis we see as a result of fast fashion. I chose to complete my degree in BA (Hons) Creative Enterprise for the textiles industry, researching how to build a sustainable business that would have little impact on the environment. I wrote my dissertation on the history of textile dyeing from the eighteenth century through to modern day and how the advent of synthetic dyes impacted the natural dye industry, looking at new technology and how we could start to lessen the devastation centuries of pollution have caused. I also began researching natural dyes and enrolled on an online certified training course to study the history of natural dyes, eco-prints and hand printing techniques.

*Do you have any inspirations or influences? This could include particular artisans, periods in history etc.*

My inspiration comes from Mother Nature herself; I love working with natural dyes because there is a touch of whimsy to the colours you can achieve. Of course, William Morris is an iconic hero for many textile artists, and I feel no different, when I read about the techniques he used and his description of how an indigo vat works I was mesmerised.

My inspiration also comes from family adventures as we love to go on camping trips, my colour names represent a life in the great outdoors such as Muddy Boots, Campfire or Hot Toddy, but I also choose names that evoke memories such as Cherished Moments and Tender Heart.

*What do you enjoy most about working with the materials that you choose to work with?*

Working with natural dyes is a lot like alchemy, you can't typically pick a colour from a pot and apply it to yarn or fabric. I always keep detailed notes and samples from every batch I dye so I can build a reference book for my colours and so I can monitor changes in results.

I love that natural dyes are very sensitive to fluctuations in PH levels and temperatures, you can easily shift the colour of a dye by adding a little dash of an acidic or alkali substance or a modifier such as iron. I love that you can use the three main historical dyes – madder, weld and indigo – to dye a rainbow by colour mixing and I just love the infinite possibilities of natural dyes.

*Please describe the tools of your craft, and how you use them.*
I work with natural dye extracts which are natural dye materials that have been dried and ground into a powder. I prefer using the dyes as an extract as it allows me to control the saturation of the colours achieved. I use large stainless-steel pots to scour, mordant and dye my yarns as the metal is non-reactive, meaning it won't affect the colours the way an aluminium pot could. I also use glass measuring jugs and a digital scale for weighing out the dye extracts.

*Describe your business. What items do you make? Do you sell items – if so, what? Do you teach courses? Describe the thing you have made that has made you most proud.*
Brambles & Me is a natural dye business that focuses on hand dyeing natural wool blends, always without nylon or synthetic materials. I like to use predominantly British Bluefaced Leicester wool as it is a hardy wool with a good staple which means it doesn't require added synthetics for strength, it is also soft enough that it can be worn next to the skin.

I prefer to source British Wool that has been spun in the UK where possible, I am currently working with a mill based in the Midlands to create a custom-blended yarn for my business. Once I dye the yarns, I rewind them to check for any imperfections and add my brand labels and photograph them to sell in my online shop.

I sell a range of repeatable colours on various yarn bases and throughout the year offer limited edition parcels inspired by seasonal events or occasions. I am most proud of my first natural yarn advent calendar from 2019. I worked closely with a knitwear designer in New York to develop a collection of accessories that would be knitted using the yarn from my advent calendar. I received wonderful feedback from customers and followers on social media.

*Please describe a typical day – as if an artist has one!*
Typically, it takes several days to create my finished hand dyed yarns. When I receive the undyed yarn from the mill it requires scouring; cleaning to remove any excess oil or lanolin from the spinning process. I then add a mordant which is a natural substance which acts like a binder to allow the yarn to absorb the natural dyes. I tie each skein with a reusable tie to make it easier to handle the skeins while working with them.

Once they have been scoured, the mordant is applied and the yarns are put on to heat for approximately an hour, the yarns then need to soak for twenty-four hours to fully absorb the mordant. The yarns are then rinsed and ready to be dyed.

I mix up the dye extracts into a dye liquor, combining colours or adding modifiers depending on the colour I aim to achieve. The yarns will then be heated again in the dye solution, this step can take a while depending on the colours and saturation required. The yarns are rinsed in cool water and hung to dip dry. Once dry, they are rewound to check for any defects and to ensure they aren't tangled, branded labels are attached and then the yarn is photographed prior to being listed in my online shop.

*What traditional 'heritage' methods do you use in your craft?*
If I am looking to dye a solid or semi-solid colour then I use the traditional vat dyeing method, the yarns are soaked to ensure the fibres are all wet

which allows the dye to penetrate to the core of each fibre strand. The heat will be applied gradually and monitored, occasionally it will be turned off to maintain an even temperature.

I also use a traditional indigo vat to dye fabrics and cellulose fibres.

*How have you adapted heritage or historic methods for the modern day?*
Traditionally the vats would have been placed over open fires and the fire would have been dampened or raised to control the temperatures, I use modern induction hobs which give instant heat and allow a much more even temperature. I am able to source more exotic dyestuffs whereas traditionally dyers would use only what they could find locally. I only source dyestuffs that are sustainable and responsibly harvested.

*What advice would you give someone starting out in your field?*
Research! There is a wealth of knowledge about natural dyes dating back centuries which covers everything from basic methods and how to shift colours.

Always be aware of fugitive dyestuffs and the temporary effects they can produce. A fugitive dye is one that is not light or washfast, meaning the colour will readily fade in the light or when washed. These colours typically come from berries, food waste and some flowers, they are beautiful although fleeting and if you intend to make a living from dyeing, I would always advise not to use dyes unless you know they will last, carry out tests and keep notes.

Website: bramblesandme.co.uk
Email: info@bramblesandme.co.uk
Social Media: @bramblesandme

## Eve Studd

*What first attracted you to your craft?*

I dabble with various artisan crafts for interests' sake but primarily I am a natural dyer and botanical printer.

Plant dyes had always been somewhere in my consciousness from early adulthood I think, part of my interest in herbs and the historic uses of plants. I promised myself one day I would look into them a bit more if I could ever find the time. It may sound odd or corny but whenever I thought about such things it felt magical, gave me a special buzz in a way that nothing else did. Another seemingly unconnected element at the time was that although I grew up in London and was a complete tomboy, so no interest in girly knitting, but whenever I got into the countryside I would collect bits of wool fleece off the wire fences and I kept it for years into adulthood, unable to throw it away and always feeling it would be useful one day. Yet I had no purpose for it and regarded myself as no good at art or crafts.

*Can you describe your journey into your craft? How did you get started? For example, do you have particular training or qualifications, or are you self-taught?*

I am a horticulturalist, and as a department manager I was sent on a stress-management day course by my employer. During the day we were encouraged to look at our work/life balance and consider what could be done to improve it. I started the day loving my job although I was aware that my life was heavily unbalanced in favour of work and travel time, but felt it was fine. At the end of the day, having seen on paper just how many hours it was all taking, I felt I hated my situation and had to do something about it. Maybe I'm just too easily influenced, everyone else seemed untroubled!

I started exploring, looking for new skills and interests which might lead in another direction or at least would enrich my quality of life at the time.

I love learning and one of the things I found was a course on natural dyes which enabled me to pick up on that long-held and unexplored interest from about twenty years previously.

I have learned through attending courses run by other experienced and skilled artisans, much reading and experimenting, but to date have no formal art qualifications as my training was in horticulture. That caused me to completely lack confidence in my work for a very long time. However, over time I discovered that people seemed to like it and so I just kept quietly going.

The most recent part of my journey has been discovering botanical printing a few years ago. Again, it seemed to develop strangely and to be a bit of a coincidence. As I have no art training, everything I learn tends to be from scratch, even simple things sometimes. Another out of the blue thing – I suddenly got the persistent urge to print, to make marks on cloth, but I knew nothing about techniques or equipment. It seemed an impulse very unlike me at the time and I don't know where it came from but it wouldn't leave me alone. My explorations led me to eco printing, which fitted completely with my existing knowledge and practice and was a natural step, becoming my main creative activity and an income strand.

*Do you have any inspirations or influences? This could include particular artisans, periods in history etc.*
I was very inspired by the artisan I first learned from, Jane Meredith of Plant Dyed Wool in Herefordshire. She is a very experienced dyer and produces beautiful work. After a couple of courses with her I started to wonder if somehow there might be a way forward for me. I had good plant knowledge and going back to my compulsive wool-saving from childhood, when I arrived on the first course there were great big baskets of wool fleece for us to use, and suddenly I knew just what I'd saved the wool for all that time. It was an amazing feeling of connection, right out of the blue. I have found inspiration in many artisans' work over the

years, but that first connection was something truly life changing and has stayed with me.

My other main source of inspiration is a particular area in the local hills near Wooler. Although we are surrounded by hills here and stunning scenery all around, there is something about that spot and it's always in my mind for its colours. Whenever we drove past on the road below I felt drawn to it for no obvious reason. Having walked it, there is an ancient hill fort on the top and for me it had a special feeling, something I've only found in one or two other places in the UK. I feel very connected to the land here.

*What do you enjoy most about working with the materials that you choose to work with?*
With the fabrics and fibres, the combination of inherent characteristics such as texture and lustre with natural colour. To date that has mostly been wool and silk, however, my practice is always moving in new directions and vegetable fibres are something I would like to explore more.

With natural dyes, I enjoy growing the dye plants I use most of which are in my organic garden, subject to the limits of our climate. One or two I have to import. I like to use the plant itself, unsurprisingly it feels more like the real thing. There's a lot to be said for natural dye extracts which seem to be increasingly popular but I like the physical connection with the living colour source and historical practice. Many dye plants are unmodified by plant breeders, so tend to offer benefits to wildlife in the garden through their flower structure. A double win in my view. I like the chunky feel in my fingers when I'm plucking the dyer's chamomile heads for example and although I have to buy in madder root as I can't grow enough for my needs, I love the subtle smell of it which persists for a long time in the dyed fibres.

*Please describe the tools of your craft, and how you use them.*
My tools are many and various, often adapted from other purposes such as my fish kettle which I use for steaming printed fabric. They're mostly pretty unglamorous too with an enormous number of pots, bins and buckets plus 'general bits', such as thermometers, pH papers, coffee filters, old stockings and other exotica!

*Describe your business. What items do you make? Do you sell items – if so, what? Do you teach courses? Describe the thing you have made that has made you most proud.*
At the moment I'm taking a break from workshops, having run them for a number of years, to allow myself more production time. At the moment, I make and sell botanically-printed silk scarves, plant dyed hand-woven wall hangings, fabric pieces, 'kitchen sink' paper and a lot of plant dyed wool fleece to needle felters, weavers etc. I've written a small introduction to plant dyes book which I hope may inspire like-minded folk. My range is always changing as inspiration leads me in one direction or another. The core elements for me are that it is a heritage skill and usually that it is plant based. I find it impossible to stick to one or two things and have to be a bit disciplined to maintain necessary focus. As a dyer though, I just want to make beautiful colour and once I've dyed or printed something I'm quite happy for someone else to make it into something. I just want to dye or print the next piece of fabric.

I'm not sure if I have a piece I'm most proud of to be honest. If it comes out well I'm happy, but then I move on to the next piece. If I kept every piece I've made and loved there'd be no room in the house by now so again I'm fairly disciplined about it. I love it, let it go and make another.

*Please describe a typical day – as if an artist has one!*
I don't have a typical day at all. My days are dictated by the season and the weather. In the winter I generally don't dye or print, I prefer to use fresh plant material and cannot get anything easily dry. So I turn round, tidy, de-stash and do the paperwork. Sometimes I might do some weaving if I have enough colours left. In the growing season I may be in the garden, weeding or harvesting or inside setting up a sequence of pots for fibre prep and dyeing so that there is a smooth flow from one to the other. If the weather turns hot I make paper.

*What traditional 'heritage' methods do you use in your craft?*
I have always tended to use historical dyes such as madder, weld, dyer's chamomile and others and use a simmering method both for dyeing and for preparing the fibres with a mordant. (A mordant holds the dye molecule on to the fibre. Most natural dyes benefit from it and for some it is essential.)

*How have you adapted heritage or historic methods for the modern day?*
Like many natural dyers, I am modifying my techniques to become more eco- friendly. When I started I would simmer almost all my mordant and dye pots as had long been the custom, but now I am moving to cold methods where I can, to reduce energy consumption. A criticism sometimes levelled at natural dyers is that we are relatively heavy on energy use, however, not all dyes need heat and mordanting can be done cold, so consumption can be substantially lowered. Another aspect has been to select the mordants I use to be more eco-friendly. In the past the use of tin or chrome was not unusual amongst dyers and I have used tin myself long ago.

*What advice would you give someone starting out in your field?*
Explore, experiment. Be thorough, understand the process and the underlying principles so you can be confident in your work. Don't believe

everything on the web, there is misinformation out there, often on quite important stuff. Go and learn from someone good.

I don't have a website at the moment but am on Facebook: Eve Studd – Cornhill Crafts and Instagram: evestudd.cornhillcrafts

## Claire Phillips, Hope Jacare

From 1988 to 1992 I attended Glasgow School of Art on the BA (Hons) Textile Design course. From 1992 to 1993 I was based at Tait and Style, Needle Felt makers on the Orkney Isles as a graduate designer. Then I worked with Judith Glue, Designer Knitwear to produce a felted knit range and run a system for outworkers. From 1994 to 1996 I worked at Donald Low in Largs, Scotland working in local jewellers and watchmakers alongside selling my handmade cards. In the period from 1993 to 2002 I started designing and making my own handmade cards. I sold my cards wholesale to many gift shops and galleries all over the UK. In 1996 (until 2002) I opened and ran 'Scoskie' gift shop and gallery in Largs.

From 2002 to 2012 I took a career break to start a family but continued to make cards for friends and family. I was also working on several design teams such as Polka Doodles, and I designed my own range of digi-stamps under Hope Jacare Designs.

However, by 2012 I started back in experimenting and dyeing in textiles, creating inspirational packs for textile designers and mixed-media artists. I exhibited in my first large textiles show at Woolfest 2013, and have never looked back!

*What first attracted you to your craft?*
I love colour and the ability to mix new colours and add colour to all types of different materials fills me with joy.

*Can you describe your journey into your craft? How did you get started? For example, do you have particular training or qualifications, or are you self-taught?*

I loved crafts and making things from a very early age, very much encouraged by my parents and grandma. I was fortunate to have a wonderful teacher within the Art department at Largs Academy such as Meg Telfer.

I studied for a BA (Hons) in textile design at Glasgow School of Art. My particular areas of interest at art school were - dyeing, yarn design, knitwear, felted knit and needle felting.

After Art school I was fortunate to gain sponsorship from the Scottish Woollen Industry. I was interviewed at my degree show for a design position at Tait and Style felt makers in the Orkney Isles and started shortly after.

*Do you have any inspirations or influences? This could include particular artisans, periods in history etc.*

I have always loved visiting art galleries and museums. Artists such as Georgia O'Keeffe, and Gustav Klimt along with sculptural textile designers such as Magdalena Abakanowicz were early influences. I was fortunate to attend a huge exhibition of Gustav Klimt's work in Brussels when I was 16.

*What do you enjoy most about working with the materials that you choose to work with?*

I love the variety of materials I am fortunate to work with. I am very much interested in all craft forms, though my heart always leads me back to textiles. There are so many more fabulous fibres readily available now compared to when I studied at Glasgow School of Art, the internet has really expanded the pallet of creative textile makers.

*Please describe the tools of your craft, and how you use them.*

Dyeing really requires very little in the way of tools, just large pots to dye on the stovetop. Smaller quantities can be dyed in a microwave. It is always very important to have separate equipment for dyeing.

I do also use carders for preparing fleece and fibres once scoured, sometimes before and sometimes post-dyeing. I can spin and weave, though my love lies with the dyeing and creating of colour.

Felting requires quite basic tools too. Needle felting – a base (sponge/ rice filled bag/woollen felted pad or brush) and a barbed needle. Wet Felting – net mesh/ bubble wrap/ towel and soap, though I do love my palm washboard.

*Describe your business. What items do you make? Do you sell items – if so, what? Do you teach courses? Describe the thing you have made that has made you most proud.*

I design and make 'creativity packs' filled with hand dyed items and notions hopefully that inspire the creative mind. Most of my packs are based on – hand dyed – yarns/threads, fabrics and fibres, eco printed – fabrics/silk papers/handmade papers and wood veneers with additions of vintage haberdashery, linen and lace, beads, Scottish tweeds and special finds (always on the look-out for new interesting elements).

In 2019 I worked on the '52 Stitched Stories' project. The 52 Stitched Stories is a community Art project with the aim of bringing creatives together, producing a postcard-sized piece of work each week. For me this was a tremendously cathartic exercise, creating a collection of pieces that is essentially a diary of my family's year. I am definitely most proud of this body of work.

*Please describe a typical day – as if an artist has one!*

I get up early to get dye pots on before the kids get up.

The school run (necessary as, though my children are older, the secondary school one has a chronic condition that means he is in and out of school each day. Most days I have four trips to and from school).

The Post Office run (I try to do Monday – Wednesday and Fridays, family life allowing).

Normally I try to dye morning or afternoon and meet friends for coffee two or three times a week to keep me sane. I can normally have my dye pots on while I am working on other new ideas.

Two or three mornings Rita comes and we chat about ideas and create new packs to be listed in the online shop.

Then there is lunch and more school runs normally.

Afternoon I try to catch up with emails/paperwork/photographing and listing new packs. Dye pots can be on bubbling. Most weeks I try to dye two or three days, however, this is partly weather dependent to get it dry.

In the evenings I tend to work while watching the telly with my husband Reuben. I have never been one to just sit. So good jobs are hand cutting fabrics/shapes, sorting fleece and pulling locks, weaving, sorting buttons. I always have a note pad with me to jot down ideas that spring to mind and make lists…..can't beat a list!

*What traditional 'heritage' methods do you use in your craft?*
Preparation of fleece is still a very traditional way. The fleece is skirted (pieces that are of no use removed) picked over, scoured by hand to remove lanolin so it can then be successfully dyed.

I am currently experimenting with natural dyeing, though this is relatively new for me.

I enjoy spinning on a drop spindle and can also use a spinning wheel for creating hand-spun yarns. Rita, who works with me, creates most of our hand-spun yarns though and owns a huge range of wheels.

*How have you adapted heritage or historic methods for the modern day?*
Microwave dyeing is a good example of modern adaptation.

I worked on a method for creating felted pebbles in the washing machine, which I believe combines the best of heritage and modern.

Weaving is a means to an end for me allowing me to weave a fabric, felt (again I have worked on a washing-machine method for this) and dye it to create a really one-off piece of fabric to work into and use in my packs and own finished pieces.

*What advice would you give someone starting out in your field?*
The most important thing about doing what I do is to be forward-thinking. Plenty of folk can copy, but its creative folk that can come up with new ideas. You have to be prepared to constantly be thinking about the next season or have ideas brewing in your mind while you are still working on the previous range. See inspiration wherever you look, seaweed on the beach, colours in clothes and interiors shops, clouds in the sky. The most important thing is to be passionate about what you do, if it becomes a chore it's not for you.

Website: www.hopejacare.co.uk

**Suzanne Dekel**
Born in the Netherlands, living and working in Israel.

*What first attracted you to your craft?*
For over twenty years I was a classically-trained musician. When I decided to quit, my creativity needed a different outlet. Eco printing, dyeing and my research about historical natural dyes have proven to be just what the doctor ordered.

*Can you describe your journey into your craft? How did you get started? For example, do you have particular training or qualifications, or are you self-taught?*

I started out with simple projects for my then new-born son; some Waldorf-style play silks dyed with fugitive berries and turmeric. I had no clue about mordants, or correct use of dyes. A small project turned into an obsession. I travelled to France to learn more, I read almost every book under the sun, and practice, practice, practice!

*Do you have any inspirations or influences? This could include particular artisans, periods in history etc.*

My favourite style was and remains the baroque period. It's what I excel in. I love the art, I love the music, I love the connection between all of it, and the books of that period are the base of most of my research and work. Books by Sir Edward Bancroft and Berthollet of the classical era are my go-to references.

*What do you enjoy most about working with the materials that you choose to work with?*

I love how my work forces me to focus, to be mindful. I love the long winding road of research, taking notes, translating, and trying (and trying again). The earthy smells of my natural dyes, the surprises they so often give. This work keeps me grounded, a gift for a lifetime.

*Please describe the tools of your craft, and how you use them.*

My cupboard is filled with little boxes full of roots, barks and exotic-smelling powders. I could not work without my scale, my little glass jars and my pH strips. Other than that you do not need much, just patience and basic knowledge.

*Describe your business. What items do you make? Do you sell items – if so, what? Do you teach courses? Describe the thing you have made that has made you most proud.*

The business side of me has evolved a lot in the last years. I started out making eco printed scarves to sell, but this was very time consuming and the more I sold, the less connected I felt. I now sell supplies for fellow dyers; dyes, mordants and un-dyed (handwoven) fabrics from all over the world. The website is a great mix between product and information, and this I am very happy about. Having the website gives me time to do my dyeing for research, eco printing and once a year a large art project where I can go wild with my craft and imagination. These projects are so satisfying, and I am very proud of the art dresses I have created. A few times a year I teach abroad, a few days teaching natural dyes and eco printing with lovely people in the south of France, or the North of Holland.

*Please describe a typical day.*

Usually I start with a good walk in the morning and some foraging if I need specific leaves for eco printing, or herbs for my tea. Then around two hours of checking orders, packing, answering questions from customers. Three times a week I work with my fabrics, I have a pretty stern schedule of projects I want to finish and research that needs to be done. I focus on one dye and combine it with different mordants and in different ratios to get a complete picture. Sometimes I have a whole month of doing a specific technique such as screen printing, or shibori. All the work needs to be catalogued and photographed, and the whole process needs to be written out. One day a week is for 'whatever I want' creative outlet, and one day a week is reserved for paperwork and other boring stuff that comes with running a business.

*What traditional 'heritage' methods do you use in your craft?*
All my work is based on what was the industrial standard of the seventeenth, eighteenth and nineteenth century. I love traditional calico printing with natural dyes especially.

*How have you adapted heritage or historic methods for the modern day?*
The 'old' ways are using tons of resources. A lot of water, a lot of mordant, a lot of dyestuff. I have made it my goals to find the right balance between using a minimum of those resources and still getting stunning dyed fabrics.

*What advice would you give someone starting out in your field?*
Patience is a virtue, pick one knowledgeable person and follow his/her way, so you do not get scattered by the tons of misinformation that's around. You cannot rush experience, if you expect great results from day one you will be in for disappointment.
Website:  www.suzannedekel.com
Instagram: @suzannedekel
Facebook Group for all things eco printing and natural dye related: BotanicalPrint Group

## Linda Illuminardi

Linda Illumanardi grew up in the mountains of Vermont, toddling behind her grandmother reciting the names of local weeds, flowers and leaves. She began eco-printing on paper, to accompany her handmade book designs (artist book limited edition Otis College, Los Angeles, CA 2001, published in Lark 500 Handmade Books, second edition, 8 collagraph plates).

Linda has a Master's degree in painting, and she loves to make impressions in each environment that she visits. She states, 'Whether in the forest or at the ocean, or in the high desert, there are always multitudes of textures, colours, and natural objects waiting to be immortalized.'

Wanting to explore further, Linda started making botanical prints on silk and wool, cotton fibres, leather and ceramics, in her quiet studio in the foothills of the Angeles National Forest.

Linda has been teaching since 1987, as well as writing curriculum and teaching from her home studio. Please see her lifestyle and work on her public Instagram account @linda.illumanardi

*What first attracted you to your craft?*
Being raised in the green mountains of Vermont with a grandmother who taught me the names of the medicinal herbs, flowers and trees, I was stunned upon arriving in Southern California twenty-one years ago to learn that not only did the average person have very little interest in knowing what they were, but that the majority of the trees were imported from around the world. Several years ago, I was introduced to the art and craft of Botanical Printing, which was the perfect excuse to wander the foothills and photograph, research and test each leaf for its colour, acid and tannin content. It has been a glorious journey, extending to printers from around the globe.

*Can you describe your journey into your craft? How did you get started? For example, do you have particular training or qualifications, or are you self-taught?*
With a Master's degree in painting and many years of throwing clay and bookbinding, I am always curious about new techniques and media, especially if it's representative of my surrounding natural environment. I first saw a brief artist presentation in a craft book with India Flint and her work with eucalyptus. Due to the abundance of imported eucalyptus here in the southlands, I became curious about which leaves

would give which colour. As I continued my explorations, I discovered that each part of the eucalyptus would give me a rather stable colour: the dried bark that blows around my yard on a windy day, the gumnuts and their caps that fall and get trampled into the soil, the branches and the flowers. For a while I wanted only to print eucalyptus on wool, and then I began to branch out and discover the many gifts that other leaves have to offer.

Overall, I am self-taught. By the time I took a class in Oregon in 2017, I had been printing for some time. The class introduced me to the joys of group bundling and sharing which opened up new possibilities in my studio. I was by then quite active in the online printing groups and must give them and their participants a heartfelt thanks and due respect as well. Their camaraderie has encouraged me to expand and grow in a multitude of ways.

*Do you have any inspirations or influences? This could include particular artisans, periods in history etc.*
Certainly I must include India's work with the eucalyptus as well as the artists that I've always studied with a keen eye: Matisse, Rothko, and of course Rauschenberg. I love the fluidity of Beatrice Wood's pottery and her influence on women in the arts, and of course the contemporary book artist Paul Johnson (England) remains close to my heart. His whimsical cut-outs and bright colours with the unusual structures are a delight to my eye and imagination. I've had the pleasure of working with Paul a couple of times, and his creativity is endless.

*What do you enjoy most about working with the materials that you choose to work with?*
The primary attraction of botanical printing for me was of course it allowed me to be outside interacting with my environment. While I was

teaching in Arizona, I was reminded by a colleague that wherever I travel, my work represents the natural environment that surrounds me. I have always been a collector of sticks, twigs, stones, feathers, shells, leaves and beautiful objects that I find on my journeys. Many of them became incorporated into my books and sometimes paintings. When I trimmed my horse's mane one day, I allowed the majority of it to be blown to the wind for the birds' nests (I have actually found some woven with my mare's hair), and then mixed some with my paint and embedded it into a large painting. I love the combinations of rusty metals and leaves and old soot-covered kettles outside over a fire. I find sticks and pipes and am a happy recipient of contractor's waste. As I've said in other interviews, being raised by my grandparents in a small village in Vermont made me very aware of reusing and the importance of having little to no waste. They were wise old souls, living humble and thoughtful lives.

*Please describe the tools of your craft, and how you use them.*
The only drawback to my craft is that in order to be safe, I must use a propane burner or induction plate outside to heat my botanical bundles. Due to the fire danger here in the foothills, an open fire is unacceptable. I'm not a fan of burning up propane or electricity, yet we all must balance our carbon footprint and make mindful choices. I live a frugal life and I would say the heat source is my Achilles heel.

I gather my leaves and often choose my 'dependables', those which I know will give me stable and beautiful colours, while always including a few 'unknowns'. I encourage my students to do the same. I have beautiful silk clothing purchased cost effectively from estate sales and local thrift and consignment shops. I have silks and cottons and linens and wool in my closet. I have beautiful papers left over from my printing/painting days, leather, scraps of wood and ceramics pots, all candidates for testing the gifts of the leaves and botanical dyes. Last month a colleague contacted me wanting a wall hanging of mine and offering a barter of many, many yards of beautiful silks she had collected from around the world. I was honoured. Such a gift.

I begin by scouring my cellulose fibres outside in soda ash and a pH 7 detergent. When the water runs clean, I dry the fabric on my line and prepare a metal mordant to ensure my prints and botanical dyes are as stable as possible. I reuse packaging that is unfortunately easy to find if I need a non-permeable barrier for the work. Plastic sheeting is wrapped on most everything that's shipped, and neighbours often save it for me instead of tossing it in the dumpster, along with their dry-cleaning bags. I reuse these until they are dried out and begin to crumble. I have a plethora of wooden, copper, steel, aluminium pipes and dowels and found sticks that my fabrics and leaves are bundled on with old strips of sheets I've torn, maintaining a tight contact for when they are immersed in the kettle or steamed.

*Describe your business. What items do you make? Do you sell items – if so, what? Do you teach courses?*
I opened Studio Good Stuff as a teaching venue here in Altadena, California in the fall of 2013, following a three-year stint in high desert Arizona where I moved to be the Department Chair of Fine Arts at an international boarding school. Studio Good Stuff began primarily as a ceramics studio which also provided a clean table and a large guillotine for bookmaking. I also have taught painting and drawing, found object assemblages, and printing on my etching press. I am very pleased to say that all students who have worked with me for portfolio preparation have been admitted to the school of their choice. When I fell in love with the botanical printing, it was easy for the studio to expand to the backyard and into a storage room out back for the additional supplies and large kettles. It was amazing that the cochineal scale insect made its home there

on a prickly pear cactus I rescued from the drought several years ago which allows me to harvest my own beautiful red dye.

As a rule, I design commissions, and often have silk clothing, scarves and wall hangings available for purchase; however, I sold out at my last open studio sale, and my teaching has dominated my schedule. Teaching itself is an art and I love to watch the variety of learners share in the joy of learning the leaves and opening the bundles. I have travelled cross-country and into Central America teaching at large venues and in private homes. It is a wonderful life to share such joy.

*Describe the thing you have made that has made you most proud.*
Hmmmm...I'm proud of every student that has passed through my life since I began teaching in 1979 straight out of high school as an instructional aide for reading disabled children in a public school system, right up to my current students who leave the botanical printing classes with their hearts filled with joy, their minds saturated with new ideas and their arms loaded with beautiful prints.

Of course I am proud of my own accomplishments as well: way back to my 200+ page thesis in graduate school and the solo exhibition of twenty-five paintings, my artist book published by Otis College in 2001, and the many positive reviews I have received. I am in love with the current assemblages I'm working on, one almost ready for display.

I must say that I am most proud of my two adult children now living beautiful, successful lives, along with my son-in-law and daughter's three beautiful sons. Nothing beats having three creative grandsons working by my side.

*Please describe a typical day.*
I begin every day with a healthy breakfast and doing my pilates and yoga routine here in my mountain studio. Often I collect leaves here in the hills

before I drive 2 miles southeast to Studio Good Stuff where I begin my average day when I am here at home. I work constantly on balancing my own work with always scouring, mordanting and prepping for classes, as well as maintaining close contact with the printers who have purchased my PDF tutorials and need assistance and feedback. I try to spend time each day participating in help threads in the printing groups, updating new classes, and communicating with venue directors. Since I am active in the local Buy Nothing group which promotes community and reduces waste, most all my sheets and linens used for dye blankets, etc., are all neighbourhood donations. Often I have to drive within a 5-mile radius to pick up these generous donations.

Currently my website is down and needs some remodelling, so I depend on social media and email for most of my communication (please see linda.illumanardi on Instagram and my email address, Lindaroars@ yahoo.com). I try to grab a quick lunch and take a hike in the afternoon with my dog and my studio partner and his two dogs.

I make a list each morning of my goals for the day which could include anything from checking and harvesting the cochineal, gathering local raw materials (oak galls, acorns, eucalyptus), prepping dye baths, maintaining contact with local dyers, and of course, there's always sitting at the computer and sealing up contracts, holding conference calls, and organizing sales and commissions.

I end each evening reviewing my accomplishments and prioritizing the tasks for the following day, and then taking my dog out by midnight to bring Tillie horse a snack before falling into bed with a good book.

*What traditional 'heritage' methods do you use in your craft?*
'Traditional heritage' in my line of work is a bit quirky since most historical documents reveal lead and chromium as mordants! Eeek! Very toxic and dangerous as we have learned. Certainly knowing and understanding my

leaves is key to my work and I rely on a variety of resources as well as my own experiments. Each region varies widely by season, and I've learned that a leaf here at my place may give something very different than a leaf 2 miles west of me. I do tend to lean toward more of a traditional naturalist approach, letting the leaves speak for themselves or exploring light mordant combinations to support their natural colours. Rarely do I soak or dye my leaves an unnatural colour. I experimented with a variety of printing techniques on the etching press for twenty years and truly have no desire currently to return to that work. I prefer my dance with nature and reading traditional as well as contemporary teachings in dyeing and botanical printing.

*How have you adapted heritage or historic methods for the modern day?*
Yes, when I read the book *A Perfect Red* by Amy Butler Greenfield, my interest in the history of cochineal was piqued. It is a marvellous historical recording of that wonderful parasitic little insect that at one point had a higher value than gold. That led me to study a variety of ancient documents and attend lectures and online events to understand the history and also the shifts in mordanting. Suzanne Tamar Dekel, a contemporary dyer in Israel is also a great resource with her generous blogs and information. I am always astounded by the online collegiality that we have developed internationally.

*What advice would you give someone starting out in your field?*
I'm confident that all of my students and those who read my replies in the help threads are well aware of my explorative style with an aim to experiment and document and learn from these studies. I don't find any value in impulsive decisions that end up in the loss of several days' work. Forethought and curiosity are key. It is most enjoyable to assist the creative process with those new learners who do the work, whether they are happy with their results or not. Doing the work matters regardless

of the medium. It gives us a starting point with something to critique, discuss, and troubleshoot. I always recommend to begin simply. Always. Don't make the leap to botanical dyes and multiple modifiers until you KNOW YOUR LOCAL LEAVES! Use a protein fibre, know how to prep simply the fabric, utilize an old hot plate outside with an enamel turkey-roaster and find a smooth stick or old pipe on which to bundle. Find a rusty object and make up a jar of rusty water and use it for your iron source.

One must always be aware of safety precautions first! Wear tight-fitting gloves, use a mask if weighing/mixing dyes and mordants, be wise about your heat source, and ALWAYS steam/immerse OUTSIDE. As they hear me say repeatedly: all of these things we use have health and safety data sheets, but there is NO data sheet for combinations of substances in the same bundle. By the time toxic vapours affect your lung tissues, it's often too late. Don't take that risk. Just because most are natural, it doesn't mean it's safe to breathe in the vapours. Don't risk that inside your home ever.

### Johanna from Potionyarns

As a former hairstylist, I dye high-quality yarns using layers of rich colour to create unique fibre that will inspire you to create your own magical masterpiece! Three years ago, I started my business, Potion Yarns, selling online and at yarn shows and festivals. My goal with my hand dyed yarns is to create rich, dimensional colours that shift and glisten from every angle. I love combining unusual colours, and creating vibrant multi-hued skeins with lustre. I'm passionate about inspiring my customers to create the life they desire, share their unique voice with the world, and continue to spread the joy and beauty of traditional handcrafts like knitting and spinning. My YouTube podcast, the Color Cauldron, celebrates beautiful fibres, teaches and inspires with tutorials, comparisons of different types of wool, pattern suggestions, and more. I hope that my yarns will inspire you to tackle that next big project, learn that new technique, try that scary new skill, and empower you to create your own magic every day! I want to help you discover and cherish the magical power and unique beauty inside yourself and encourage you to share that with the world!

*What first attracted you to your craft?*
As a lifelong crafter, I had fallen in love with yarn and making things with my hands. I love the way handmade products have such life, such soul, and such character. There's a whole story involved with each piece! As a hairstylist who specialized in bright, vivid hair colours, I was already obsessed with colour and creating moods using the way we perceive shades and hues. It was a natural fit.

*Can you describe your journey into your craft? How did you get started? For example, do you have particular training or qualifications, or are you self-taught?*
My training is as a master colourist. I started as a hairstylist, specializing in unique, rainbow colours, and had been doing that for over ten years by the time I tried dyeing yarn. So I was trained in colour theory, chemistry, and had real-world experience with how different people perceive colours, how to mix and create colours, etc. But my specific yarn and fibre dyeing expertise has been mostly self-taught, hands on experience. I did take an online class from another indie dyer when I was first starting out that helped me hone my individual style. Most of the classes I've taken have been related to running a business, photographing my work, etc.

*Do you have any inspirations or influences? This could include particular artisans, periods in history, etc.*
I find inspiration everywhere! I've had a lot of fun creating yarn colours that were inspired by hair colours I created for my clients in the salon.

It's fun to see the yarn next to the hair that inspired it! As a lifelong lover of vintage style and history, I love using old movies from the studio era, jazz music, and vintage clothing as inspiration. A lot of my ideas come from books I've enjoyed, movies I love, or mythology. I create colours that evoke the stories and moods I feel when I read or listen to them. I can get great ideas just about anywhere: some of my favourite places to go when I'm feeling stuck is the park by my house, the Nelson-Atkins Art Museum in my city, or the botanical garden.

*What do you enjoy most about working with the materials that you choose to work with?*
I really love working with yarn and fibre because it's so soft and feels amazing in your hands! I love the excitement and joy I feel when I'm creating colours and I get to see it all coming together.

*Please describe the tools of your craft, and how you use them.*
For the actual dyeing, I use a variety of techniques but they all involve some kind of water, heat and acid to set the dyes. Most commonly, I use citric acid to help the dyes stick to the wool permanently, but I also use vinegar from time to time. I actually source most of my equipment from restaurant supply stores and it really is like cooking: I use big stock pots for immersion dyeing, catering pans for multi-coloured skeins, and induction burners to heat the yarn and water.

*Describe your business. What items do you make? Do you sell items – if so, what? Do you teach courses? Describe the thing you have made that has made you most proud.*
I hand-dye yarn and fibre and sell it to artists and crafters who create magical projects from my products. I mostly sell online, but also at fibre festivals and events, as well as wholesaling to yarn shops. Most of my

business is hand dyed yarn, but I am starting to add spinning fibre to my dyed creations so people can spin their own yarn using my beautiful colour combinations. I don't currently teach anything; but I do produce a free podcast on YouTube and occasionally will have a tutorial on that. We also talk about different types of wools and how to use them, methods for knitting socks and shawls, how to choose colours for a project, and lots more.

I take great pride in my work and love creating all the beautiful colours. But the thing I'm most proud of creating is my self-sustaining business because that was something that never came naturally for me and seemed the most challenging to me. Overcoming my fears, anxiety, lack of finances, experience, etc. to build a business from the ground up has been really amazing.

The dyed creation I am most proud of would probably be my sock blanks. Hand-painting sock blanks is a time consuming process, and quite different than the styles of yarn and fibre dyeing I usually do. It has taken a lot of trial and error and I'm still honing and perfecting my technique; but last year I painted a sock blank to look like our solar system, with planets, and a sun, and swirling colours evoking deep space. It was the most intricate thing I've created so far.

*Please describe a typical day.*
Part of what I love about this business is there isn't a typical day! But for a day of dyeing, I do have a routine of sorts. I usually select the yarns or fibres I'm planning to start working on the night before and put them in pans or buckets of water to soak. In the morning, I prep my dye space with towels, clearing counters to make as much room as possible, getting out my measuring tools and scale, and start heating water. Typically, I do between three and five batches of yarn or fibre at a time, and each batch will be between 3-6 skeins, depending on the

technique I'm using. I'll usually apply colour to one batch, then while it's setting, move on to the second, etc. I'm currently working out of my kitchen, saving up for a dedicated dye space in my home; so I'll have a couple of pans going on the stovetop, a couple more in the oven, and another one or two on induction burners on my countertop. Once I can build the space I'm designing, I'll move to all induction burners and a couple of food warmers to recreate the oven and stove combo but in an easier to clean/control environment.

As I work, I add more yarns to soak if I think I have time to keep going. Most of my yarns go through multiple pots of colour, but once they are completely finished and the dyes are set, I remove the yarn from the heat and let it cool; then begin an arduous rinsing process. Excess water is spun out gently, then they are hung to dry (outside in nice weather, in my basement or wherever I can find space inside when it's not temperate out). Then I begin the long, tedious process of cleaning up, being sure to bleach all my equipment and surfaces to remove dye residue or spills.

On days when I'm not dyeing, I'm usually taking photos of yarn, twisting and prepping skeins for sale, labelling and tagging, updating the website, responding to customers online, posting on social media, doing inventory, and taking care of my son and our house.

*What traditional 'heritage' methods do you use in your craft?*
Dyeing yarn and fibre has been around for millenia. Natural dyes were the only way to do it for centuries, but with the introduction of acid dyes (the kind I use), options for colours expanded. I still consider it a heritage craft to take undyed yarn and fibre and colour it by hand. It's the small batch, artisan dyeing that really reconnects us to our roots and centuries past. Even though dyeing is the focus of my business, I personally enjoy knitting and spinning for pleasure, and I use both crafts to showcase my creations to customers, connect with people online and at events, etc. It's

really fun for people to see my creations using my yarns and it gives them an idea of how they will look when used.

*How have you adapted heritage or historic methods for the modern day?*
Acid dyes are relatively modern. But the thing that I use the most that is completely new is the internet. As a primarily online business, that is my bread and butter, so it's essential for me to connect with customers using the internet and modern technology. I love that we can honour the past with traditional crafts like spinning, crochet, etc. yet do it in a way that is relevant and fun for modern audiences. I use the internet not to only sell and conduct business; I join Facebook groups with like-minded crafters to talk about our love of fibre, I post on social media so people can see my products and processes, I participate in virtual knit nights, host a YouTube podcast about fibre crafts, and am able to find knitwear designers, other dyers, yarn shops and others to collaborate with. Most of my customers are quite active online and connect with other yarn lovers and businesses like mine. It's great to be able to still make sales at 3 am through my online shop!

*What advice would you give someone starting out in your field?*
Grow incrementally. Don't feel like you have to do it all at once. It's better to do two things really consistently than ten things haphazardly. I'd also say the best way to learn is by doing, so allow yourself to play and practise and trust that you will develop your own style. It's not good to try to copy other people's work: each dyer has their own style and techniques. You can learn from others for sure, but you'll find a way to put your own unique spin on it and that's the beauty of hand dyeing: each of us is unique and no one else can ever quite capture or perfectly copy our individual products. So don't try too hard to be like others, but find your own way of doing things.

Website: www.potionyarns.com/
Facebook: www.facebook.com/PotionYarns/
Instagram: www.instagram.com/potionyarns/?hl=en
YouTube: www.youtube.com/channel/UC0hBEtd_AKzMke5dWtctKmQ
Pinterest: www.pinterest.com/potionyarns/

## Karen Walthinsen

*What first attracted you to your craft?*
Honestly, I didn't ever think I would be interested in dyeing. Several years ago, I was invited to join two other women I had met in Qatar to open an Etsy shop selling children's knits. We were terribly international – one in the USA, one in Australia and me in Norway. Although that shop gradually faded away, I became quite close over the internet with my friend in Australia. At that point she had been dyeing and encouraged me to give it a try. I was intent on natural dyeing and, living in a Norwegian forest, I started foraging for dye materials. I tried lichen, heather, various mushrooms, kitchen scraps, plant roots, flowers, and basically experimented with anything I had a hunch might give me colour. I even cooked up the Christmas tree needles. Somehow this gave me a very powerful, magical feeling. I thought of myself as a dyeing wizard.

*Can you describe your journey into your craft? How did you get started? For example, do you have particular training or qualifications, or are you self-taught?*
Ever since I was a child, growing up in the days when we read books and played outside, I have been attracted to anything to do with fibre. It probably all started with one of those pot-holder looms and little needlepoint kits. By 6, I was crocheting, by 12 it had been cross-stitch for years and I began to sew my own clothes. At the age of 15, I spent a

summer visiting various relatives in Norway and that was when I learned to knit. It was, and still is, such a normal thing to do in Norway, that as I hopped from family to family, there was always someone who could help. Needless to say, that first sweater was an interesting study in wonky gauge, but it got me started.

*Do you have any inspirations or influences? This could include particular artisans, periods in history, etc.*

For me it's simply the thought of dyeing being such an old craft. Living in Norway, it's fascinating to think about what the Vikings used to dye their clothes and what colour meant. Simply the colour of one's clothing could tell a lot about one's place in social hierarchy. I'm always fascinated to read about other uses of dye, for instance in the ink used for illuminated manuscripts of the middle ages. I'm also quite inspired by those who keep tradition alive. Especially in the fall, I tend to see a multitude of posts on social media of the dyeing experiments of Norwegians.

*What do you enjoy most about working with the materials that you choose to work with?*

I love the unpredictability when I'm in an experimentation phase. Sometimes what seems to be the most unpromising combination turns out to have the most beautiful and surprising result.

*Please describe the tools of your craft, and how you use them.*

I keep it quite simple. I have only three old pots, one induction burner and lots of jars and glasses. Jars often contain lichen that has been soaking for months. Glasses I use for mixing up acid dyes. I do things in small batches. I don't want the novelty to wear off and turn my little side-business into something I dread.

*Describe your business. What items do you make? Do you sell items – if so, what? Do you teach courses? Describe the thing you have made that has made you most proud.*

I have an online business and occasionally, when my schedule permits, I do fibre festivals. I sell yarn, kits and I am trying to get my own designs out there. Sometimes I gear my dyeing technique to specific designs. Just recently, I must say, I'm quite proud of a kit I put together with my own design. It has a strong concept and story particularly in keeping with the current world situation. If it gives hope and provides solace for even one person, then it will have been worth the blood, sweat and tears to make it happen.

*Please describe a typical day.*

I work as a violinist in a symphony orchestra, so my days usually begin with a rehearsal. After that, depending on my 7-year-old's schedule, we may have after-school activities or it's home to relax, do some practising. It's after my son goes to bed that I do most of my dyeing during the week. Our weekly schedule is not as strenuous as it tends to be for orchestras in other parts of the world, so I am often free for three days of the week. Fridays are probably the most productive. I begin soaking my yarn the night before (usually after playing a concert) and once I deliver my son to school, I am free to get to work. Some days I have a clear plan, dyeing colourways that I often repeat. Other days I'm inspired to just play with the colours and see what happens. Sometimes I have a plan. Sometimes I don't. I must admit that I often stay up MUCH too late because I get on a roll.

*What traditional 'heritage' methods do you use in your craft?*

Fermenting materials (such as lichen) over longs periods of time, drying mushrooms for later use and manipulating colour by immersing yarn in baths containing, for example, iron water.

*How have you adapted heritage or historic methods for the modern day?*
There's something very special about natural dyeing. The colours feel so alive, but what I really missed was taking it one step further and making the colours mingle together and take on a life of their own. What I have seldom seen is naturally dyed variegated yarn. I'll never forget my very first experiment. I put jars of dye baths from various materials in a large pot filled with water and strung the yarn from jar to jar. After letting it cook for a while, I looked in and didn't see much of anything, but I decided to let it sit and cool outside overnight. The next morning I lifted the lid with great anticipation, but everything looked a disappointing grey. Still, I took the skein out and went to rinse it in clean water and I will never forget that moment. The colour just leapt out of the yarn. Three or four different dye materials had resulted in this amazing set of colours that went together so beautifully.

I don't do as much natural dyeing anymore – it is time consuming and the results are a bit unreliable. I have turned to acid dyes for the most part, but even with those, I have recently delved into dyeing non-superwash yarn with the traditional Norwegian 'kofte' in mind. A kofte is a colour-work cardigan or pullover using motifs which often identify it with a particular part of the country. Norwegians tend to use a lot of colour, but only solid colours. I'm attempting to merge my style of semi-solids or very subtle variegation to be used in knitting traditional kofte patterns.

*What advice would you give someone starting out in your field?*
In a way, the best advice I can give someone is just jump in there and get your hands dirty. As long as you create a product with that integrity, there is no one way you can go wrong. It's all about experimentation.

*Chapter 10*

# Have a go at Eco Printing at Home

If you have been inspired by reading about the artisans featured in this book, why not try your hand at eco-dyeing? This lovely craft takes plant materials and prints onto fabric with gorgeous effects. You can use many plants from your garden, or leaves gathered on a walk to try eco printing yourself.

Eco printing works well on silk or wool fabric. Other natural fibres are used effectively (you can see examples in the artisans section of this book) but start with silk or wool, because the plant dyes cling best to protein fibres, and you want to make your first attempt as easy as possible to avoid frustration.

You will need:

A length of natural or pale silk or woollen fabric
Digital scales
Alum
Plastic sheeting
Stainless steel pan
Plant materials (see below)
Water
Heat source for water
Dye material for under dyeing (either dye plant materials or prepared
    natural dyes – see suppliers list at the end of this volume)
Length of plastic such as sheeting for wrapping or a cut-down
    bin bag
Stick
Cotton string

Face mask (I use N95 masks with a kind of metal strip across the inside which moulds around my nose – it's very important that ALL dyeing is done in ventilated space and wearing a mask and gloves for safety purposes. You do NOT want to breathe in alum powder, micro-fine dye powder or any other dyeing materials that could potentially harm you.)

1. Start by washing your fabric with a mild washing liquid to remove any coatings that may have been added during manufacture. This process is called *scouring*.

2. *Mordant* your fabric. That means applying a solution to prepare the fabric to accept the dye (you would use this in dip dyeing too). *Mordant* makes dyed fabric colour and light fast so your dyeing does not fade or wash out. Alum (potassium aluminium sulphate) is readily available online and in some craft outlets. You need 12g of alum for every 100g of silk or wool fabric. Don't guess; weigh them out – that way you will get the most satisfying results.

   Measure the amount of alum you need and mix it with a little warm water to make a solution. Set it to one side where you won't knock it over (trust me – I learned this the hard way!). Fill a stainless steel pot with water (so it won't stain) and bring it to the boil. Add the alum solution carefully to the water. Now, I keep separate pans especially for dyeing and I think that is good practice for hygiene and safety purposes. Add the textile to the water and turn off the heat – you don't want to spoil your fabric by boiling it up like an old rag! Let the fabric steep for about an hour – it needs to be cool before it is handled anyway. Gently squeeze to remove excess moisture but don't wring out the fabric – you want the mordant to stay where it is.

3. Here is an exciting optional step – you can under dye the fabric with a natural dye for a lovely end result. Use a light shade of colour at first and experiment later with different effects. To do this, make a

*dye bath*. There are lots of ways to do this with different materials and natural, ready-prepared dyes – you can follow the instructions on the packet when you buy them. An easy starter idea is to use plants such as Dyer's Weld to create a simmer bath (some natural dyes have a more complicated process; indigo requires fermentation to create a reduction dye vat and madder is cold water dyed – there is time to investigate those processes later when you have some experience).

4. This is the exciting bit (or at least one of the exciting bits. I'm a plant nerd, so this excites me very much indeed). Go out and collect your plant materials! So – what works best? Some of them may be in your garden already – or at least be available in areas nearby.

Leaves:

- Birch
- Alder
- Chestnut
- Oak
- Apple
- Cherry
- Plum
- Peach
- Maple
- Ginkgo
- Sumac
- Eucalyptus
- Willow
- Dye plant leaves (madder, woad, weld)
- Pine needles.

You can also collect flowers, seeds, bark, pods, herbs, weed roots – and lots more. Experiment and find out what happens. Keep notes as you experiment because you will then have a record of what works and what does not, and you can tinker with your results. I suspect if you are reading this book that you might be one of those people like me who is unable to go for a walk without collecting natural treasures like coppery autumn leaves – your time has come!

Back at home, wipe off your materials making sure bugs are safe and that the plant material is not muddy.

5.  Lay your plastic out on the table. Lay the wet, already mordanted fabric on top of the plastic.
6.  The next stage is exciting! Arrange your collected treasures on half of the fabric (measuring lengthways). Then fold the half of the fabric without plant treasures on, over the laid out material. In that way, the plant material will be trapped between two layers of fabric.
7.  Lay your stick on one end of the folded fabric. Roll up your fabric around the stick, with the plant treasures inside. Wrap it tightly and then wrap the bundle in string to hold it tightly closed.
8.  Now you are going to steam your bundle. I use a fish kettle as it is long and takes large scarves etc. Equally, you could use a slow cooker or a crock pot. Use a small amount of water on a low setting and make sure the fabric is NOT in the water – it needs to be on a steam basket because it just needs to be steamed. Steam your bundle on low for 3 hours.
9.  Now comes the hard part. After 3 hours, turn off the pot and leave the pot to cool – I leave it overnight to let the colours develop. If I can bear it I try to leave my bundles for about 25-30 hours.
10. Now the best part! Remove the bundle and snip the string. Unwrap your lovely surprise, and carefully remove the plant material. There

will be lots of patterns and colours! One of the best things is, you are never quite sure of the result you are going to get.

11. Rinse the fabric through by hand with mild soap, then a gentle rinse water with a spoonful of vinegar to restore the pH. A final rinse with cool clear water and you are done! Admire your results, and hang your fabric to dry.

*Chapter 11*

# Planning a Dye Garden

Now that you've read through this book and understand the history of dyeing, both natural and industrial, I hope that some among you may be inspired to try it out yourself. If that is the case, then I've prepared a section here to help you get started with a dye garden so you know what you can grow, what you might already be growing and how you can organise your garden to give you the colours you need.

The best way to start is with some basic colour theory. The likelihood is that you're going to want to have a variety of colours at your disposal and it's equally as likely that, as different climates will support plants differently, that you may not have the same options as someone else reading this. With that in mind, we can start by planning out plants for red, blue and yellow. These primary colours will allow you, with time and a little creativity, to produce a wide variety of shades. The big advantage to this approach is that it requires less dedicated space than trying to find a plant for the individual colours you might want if they fall into the secondary or tertiary colours.

*Plants you can use to make blue dyes.*
**Woad:** Don't be fooled by its yellow flowers, *Isatis Tinctoria* has long been used to create blue dye. Although less concentrated than indigo it's a good choice as it produces a large amount of seeds to be replanted after each harvesting year.

**Indigo:** *Indigofera Tinctoria* also known as 'true indigo' is a purple flowering plant whose leaves can be processed to create a strong blue dye. Although it gives a higher concentration of dye than woad, it's more suited to warmer climates and so may not be your 'go to' choice.

**Japanese Indigo:** *Persicaria Tinctoria* or 'Dyers Knotweed' can also be used to produce blue dyes and it's the green leaves of the plant, rather than the pink or white flowers which contain the colour you're looking for. These plants will need to be protected from frosts and shouldn't be confused with the plant 'Japanese Knotweed' which is a weed which will spread quickly through your garden if not removed.

*Plants you can use to make red dyes.*
**Madder:** *Rubia Tinctorum* is well-known as being able to produce a strong red colour sometimes known as 'Turkey Red'. It can grow upwards of a metre in height and the dye is extracted from the roots of the plant rather than the leaves or stems. In order to extract enough colour to be used, you may need to wait until the second year of the plant's life cycle so that the roots have grown thick enough.

**Lady's Bedstraw:** *Galium Verum* is from the same plant family as madder, known as 'Rubiaceae'. Its roots can also be used to create a red dye colour, although the roots of this plant contain less than its cousin. However, it holds one advantage over madder in that the plant stems can also be used to produce a yellow dye, meaning that you get two dyes for the price of one from this plant but may need to grow it in larger quantities to achieve the same amount of dye.

**Sorrel:** *Rumex Acetosa* while better known as a sharp-tasting plant that can be used to add a little bite to soups, this common herb's roots can also be used to produce a red dye. It doesn't take up a lot of space and has the benefit of being multi-use so it doesn't necessarily need to be added to a separate section of the garden reserved for dye plants either.

*Plants you can use to make yellow dyes.*
**Weld:** *Reseda Luteola* also known as 'Dyer's Rocket' has been used to achieve yellow dye shades since the Iron Age and can be used on a range of fabrics. Once fruits are showing on the plant, the colour stored within it starts to fade so it's one to cut early.

**Dyer's Chamomile:** *Cota Tinctoria* can be used to create bright yellow and orange shades. It's hardy and able to grow in poor soils and so even if you don't have the most productive beds to grow in, you should still be able to get some results from this plant. Although it doesn't share the qualities of German or Roman Chamomile in terms of its culinary uses for teas etc., it's a useful dyer's flower and has the advantage that its bright yellow flowers are reminiscent of sunflowers and will add some colour to your dye plants.

**Goldenrod:** *Solidago* like madder can grow to around one and a half metres in height and so might not be the right choice for those with limited space. That being said, cutting the yellow flowers when they're new will produce beautiful yellows. The flowers can be dried and used later although they will be less effective than when used fresh. Similarly, if the flowers are cut from the plant later in their life cycle, they will yield less dye than when first flowered.

It's worth remembering, now that we have our primary colours picked out, that natural dyeing is not an exact science. Some plants will produce much stronger dyes than others for example and as such they might overpower the dye from another when you try to combine them. This means that getting the shades you want will, at times, require quite a bit of experimentation and that at times the results may be more difficult to replicate.

Bear in mind the journey can at times be as much fun as the destination. The process of experimentation of course can bring about some fantastic results, and you will be able to discover a wonderful range of shades while on the way to the colours in your head.

The plants above will flower at different times of the year and are a mixture of perennials, annuals and biennials and it is by no means an exhaustive list of the plants available to you. I would urge you to do some further research into how they would be affected by the climate of the area you live as well as the quality of your soil, and the amount of space you have available to you. It is also worth considering how often you plan to dye fabrics, in terms of whether you will use plants when they become available to you or whether you would want to store materials to be used year round as this may affect your choices.

You can find seeds available for some of the plants mentioned here within the suppliers section of this book.

# Directory of Suppliers

*T*hese suppliers can provide you with everything you need, from tools to delicious fibres.

### Botanical Inks

www.botanicalinks.com/ – Botanical Inks offer a selection of courses from their artisan studio in Bristol including private tuition which can be booked through their website. They have also recently produced a book *Botanical Inks: Plant-To-Print Dyes, Techniques and Projects* which shows you ways to produce your own natural dyes in an environmentally stable way.

### DT Crafts

www.dtcrafts.co.uk/ – Debbie and Pete Tomkies have been running DT Crafts since 2005 and the Cheshire based family business offers a variety of textile courses including hand dyeing while the online store make a range of natural dyes including the US based Botanical Colours liquid dyes.

### Dylon

www.dylon.co.uk/en/home.html – Dylon have been in business since 1946 as 'Dyes of London' and today produce a large range of dye colours to choose from whether you're looking to dye by hand or using a machine.

### Empress Mills

www.empressmills.co.uk/ – This Lancashire based company has a wide selection of colours available for acid dyes as well as a range of Procion dyes that can be used for cold water dyeing of natural fibres such as silks.

## Ewe and Ply

https://eweandply.co.uk/ – As well as bricks and mortar locations in Shrewsbury and Oswestry, Ewe and Ply operate an online store where you can purchase dyes, mordants and book places on workshops to be held on location.

## George Weil

www.georgeweil.com/ – A large arts and crafts supplier, George Weil supply a variety of natural and non-natural dye colours, while their bookshop contains a collection of books relating to dyeing, both its history and techniques that may be useful for you.

## Handprinted

https://handprinted.co.uk/ – Although more focused on print based work as the name suggests, this organisation based in Bognor Regis supplies a range of dyes, dyeing equipment and runs some workshops on the subject also.

## Handweavers Studio

www.handweavers.co.uk/ – The Handweavers Studio & Gallery in London offers both natural and non-natural dyes, equipment, a variety of books relating to the subject and a workshop list covering dyeing amongst other things.

## The Dye Shop

www.thedyeshop.co.uk/ – Running since 2009, this family business offers a huge colour selection of dyes and their website features a handy 'which dye guide' that helps you choose the dye that's best suited to the type of fabric you're using.

### Vinyl Dye

www.vinyldye.co.uk/ – This website was set up to provide dye products that could be used on plastics in an effort to spruce up the usual white or grey plastic products found at home. Their dyes work by bonding to the plastic itself changing its colour by 'melting' into the product without damaging it through multiple coats. They also offer dyes suitable for use on satin, leather and even suede with their website providing some useful guides on how to use the dyes and what you use them for.

### Wild Colours

www.wildcolours.co.uk/ – Birmingham based Wild Colours is run by textile artist Teresinha Roberts and sells natural dye extracts for a range of colours, shipped worldwide in powder form, you can also purchase woad, mordants, indigo dyes and book to attend workshops via the website.

### Wingham Wool Work

www.winghamwoolwork.co.uk/Rotherham based Wingham Wool Work offer a wide range of natural dyes from Kraft Kolours range as well as books on the subject of dyeing. They also have a calendar on their website with a list of courses and events for the year.

### Training Courses

www.handmadetextilesbycaroline.co.uk/429655766 – Caroline Nixon offers a range of workshops taking place in multiple locations and countries, her courses detail techniques for eco printing as well as the use of natural dyes.

https://naturalfabricdyeing.com/ – Justine Aldersey-Williams, owner of The Wild Dyery runs workshops from her studio in The Wirral and also offers online study in natural fabric dyeing through her website.

# Useful Books and Websites

Behan, Babs, *Botanical Inks: Plant-to-Print Dyes, Techniques and Projects* (Quadrille Publishing Ltd, 2018)

Booth, Abigail, *The Wild Dyer: A guide to natural dyes & art of patchwork & stitch* (Kyle Books, 2017)

Burgess, Rebecca, *Harvesting Color: How to Find Plants and Make Natural Dyes* (Artisan Division of Workman Publishing, 2011)

Callahan, Gail, *Hand Dyeing Yarn and Fleece: Dip Dyeing, Hand-Painting, Tie-Dyeing, and Other Creative Techniques* (Storey Publishing LLC, 2010)

Dean, Jenny, *Wild Colour: How to Make and Use Natural Dyes* (Mitchell Beazley, 2018)

Desnos, Rebecca, *Botanical Colour at your Fingertips* (Self-published, 2016)

Duerr, Sasha, *The Handbook of Natural Plant Dyes: Personalize Your Craft with Organic Colors from Acorns, Blackberries, Coffee, and Other Everyday Ingredients* (Timber Press, 2011)

Finlay, Victoria, *Colour: Travels Through the Paintbox* (Sceptre publishing, 2003)

Hawksley, Lucinda, *Bitten by Witch Fever: Wallpaper & Arsenic in the Nineteenth-Century Home* (Thames & Hudson, 2016)

Johansen, Linda, *Fabric Dyers Dictionary: The Only Dyeing Book You'll Ever Need* (C&T, 2010)

Matthews David, Alison, *Fashion Victims: The Dangers of Dress Past and Present* (Bloomsbury Visual Arts, 2001 edition)

McLaughlin, Chris, *A Garden To Dye For: How To Use Plants From The Garden to Create Natural Colors for Fabrics & Fibers* (St. Lynn's Press, 2014)

Vejar, Kristine, *The Modern Natural Dyer: A Comprehensive Guide to Dyeing Silk, Wool, Linen, and Cotton at Home* (STC Craft, 2015)

**Useful Websites**

Bitten By Witch Fever: Wallpaper and Arsenic in the Nineteenth-Century Home. www.charteredinvestor.org/1751eb/bitten-by-witch-fever-wallpaper-and-arsenic-in-the-nineteenth-century-home.pdf

Creating Lichen Dyes (Letharia Vulpina or Wolf Lichen) www.instructables.com/Creating-Lichen-Dyes-Letharia-vulpina-or-Wolf-Lich/

Rosalie's Medieval Woman - Dyes and Colours. https://rosaliegilbert.com/dyesandcolours.html

Sir William Henry Perkin and the Coal-Tar Colours. www.victorianweb.org/science/perkin.html

The Buggy Truth about Natural Red Dye | JSTOR Daily. https://daily.jstor.org/the-buggy-truth-about-natural-red-dye/

# Glossary

**Alizarin (synthetic):** a synthetic dye created in 1868. It was synthesized from coal tar. Synthetic alizarin could be produced at a quarter of the price of the natural dye.

**Alum:** a type of metal salt used to mordant (allow dye to bond) with fibres.

**Brasilwood:** the East India tree yielded Brasilwood, which could be used to extract a purple dye.

**Carmine:** a red dye extracted from the cochineal beetle.

**Coal Tar:** coal tar is a viscous liquid by-product of the production of gas and coke. By 1900, more than fifty compounds had been synthesized using coal tar.

**Cochineal:** a type of beetle used to produce red dye.

**Coreopsis:** a type of daisy-like flower that can be used to produce yellow, orange and brown dyes.

**Drydye:** a special pressurized carbon dioxide process which negates the need for water usage in the dye process.

**Dyer's Rocket:** the common name for weld. It yields a yellow dye.

**Dyer's Greenwood:** a plant used to yield green dye.

**Finishing** (textiles): finishing was the term used to describe what happened after yarn and cloth was created, and encompassed bleaching, dyeing and printing.

**Formaldehyde:** a strong-smelling, toxic gas used to allow better saturation of dyes and inks to colour textiles.

**Fustic:** a dye extracted from a tree from the Mulberry family. It yields yellows, golds and oranges.

**Gum Arabic:** a natural gum used in printing textiles.

**Indigo:** a blue dye produced from the *Indigofera Tinctoria* plant.

**Kermes:** a beetle used to yield red dye.

**Logwood:** logwood chips yield strong, vibrant purple dye.

**Madder:** a root that yields red dye.

**Mauve Measles:** Aniline purple, a synthetic dye, caused 'Mauve Measles' – a nasty rash which irritated and inflamed the skin.

**Mordant:** mordants are used to help dye to bond with fibres. They can be weak organic acids such as tannic acid and acetic acid. They can also be metal salts such as alum, ferrous sulphate and copper sulphate.

**Murex shells:** Tyrian Purple was extracted from several *Murex* shellfish. Apart from the main source, *Murex brandaris*, the purple fluid could also be extracted from *Murex trunculus*.

**Oil of vitriol:** in the 1700s, sulphuric acid was known as *oil of vitriol*.

**Orchil:** Orchil was a violet or red dye produced using lichens.

**Polychromic:** some natural dyes are *polychromic*, they have the property of yielding different colours with different mordants. Cochineal and madder are examples.

**Pre-mordant:** when textiles are soaked and simmered in mordant solution before the dyes are applied.

**Procion dyes:** these dyes are able to bond directly to the fibres of the fabric they were applied to, avoiding colour run. They are perfect for tie-dyeing.

**Sandalwood (Red Sandalwood):** a wood used to produce a range of red and brown dyes.

**Scheele's Green:** a green dye created by Carl Scheele, a chemist from Sweden, in 1775. It was produced by combining arsenious oxide with a sodium carbonate solution. The arsenic made the pigment toxic.

**Shibori:** a traditional Japanese method of dyeing that uses thread to isolate points on the fabric being dyed to create a 'tie-dye' effect.

**Tartaric acid:** Tartaric acid is a natural acid that occurs in fruits such as grapes. It is sometimes used in dyeing by adding it to the alum mordanting process. It protects and softens fibres and brightens the shades of colours.

**Tie-dyeing:** A method of tying fabric before dyeing it, to create a pattern.

**Tyrian purple:** Tyrian purple was a dye made from the shells of the *Mediterranean Murex*.

**Woad:** woad is a yellow-flowered plant. The dried leaves produce a blue dye.